Aladdin

A Pantomime

Norman Robbins

Samuel French - London
New York - Toronto - Hollywood

CHARACTERS

Abanazar, the Magician
The Slave of the Ring
Aladdin
Widow Twankey, his mother
Wishee Washee, a local layabout
The Grand Vizier
The Emperor Chow Mein, Ruler of all China
Princess Badroulbador, his daughter
So-Shy, her lady-in-waiting
The Genie of the Lamp
The Mummy
Chorus of Citizens, Laundryworkers, Courtiers, Spirits
    of the Cave, Guards, Chinese Policemen, *etc.*
Chorus of Babes

AUTHOR'S NOTE

This version of the Aladdin story was first performed at the Grand Pavilion Theatre, Porthcawl, Mid Glamorgan, on 26th December 1980 for the season, and was directed by myself.

To enable it to be performed by amateur companies, I have simplified the staging to suit the average church hall or small theatre. Lighting, special effects and properties have been kept to a minimum, and although songs and dances I leave to the discretion of the director, I have prepared a list of music suggestions which is obtainable from me, c/o Samuel French Ltd.

Knowing the demands of the amateur stage, I have expanded the cast numbers by two, but apart from that, you have what we had.

Running time is about two hours and a quarter, providing the pace is brisk. Costumes and scenery should be as stylized as possible.

PRODUCTION NOTE

In Act 1, Scene 2, it is best if *all* characters involved are supplied with hot-water bottles. It is less messy for performers *and* the rest of the company during later scenes.

In Act 1, Scene 5, the washing machine is simply a four-sided box painted white with an "observation window" painted on the front. Make sure it is large enough to accommodate Wishee when he falls in, and do provide an exit hole in the cloth behind it. His costume change is fairly quick.

For
Myrtle and Cliff Devenish

ACT I

Beneath the Great Sphinx in Egypt

A lane cloth depicting a huge hall of Egyptian design, dimly lit in shades of blue and green. The sinister figure of Abanazar, an evil magician, is C, his left hand held slightly below his face at an angle in order to display the large stoned ring he wears on his finger, and his right hand a little above shoulder level, fingers splayed as though to cast a spell on the ring. A green spotlight illuminates him

Abanazer (*hoarsely*) O magic ring ... fashioned by the spells of Egypt's ancient gods ... I call upon your aid. Tell me that which I ... Abanazar ... most powerful of all magicians ... desire to know. The whereabouts of the Magic Lamp ... the Lamp I *must* have to make me ruler of all the world. (*He gives a harsh laugh and rubs the ring*)

There is a flash and the Slave of the Ring appears

Slave I am the Slave of the Ring, O master. Here to do thy bidding. What is thy wish? (*He bows his head*)

Abanazer (*snarling*) The Magic Lamp. Where is it? Speak, I command you.

Slave In a cavern deep, below the ground,
The Lamp lies hidden. Safe and sound.

Abanazer (*impatiently*) Yes, yes, but where? Where?

Slave Near a mountain top in a foreign land.
But master, try to understand,
You who are wicked may not make your way
To the head of *that* cavern. Outside you must stay.

Abanazer (*snarling*) What?

Slave If anyone evil inside it should tread,
In the blink of an eyelid, he'll surely be dead.
Another soul must play the questing part,
An honest boy. Fearless. What's more, pure of heart.
Without *his* help, master, the Lamp remains
Outside your grasp always, in spite of your pains.

Abanazer (*raging*) Ten thousand curses. Where in *this* day and age can I find a boy as innocent as that?

Slave I know of but *one* (though more is the pity)
He dwells in far off Peking City.

Aladdin is his given name,
A youth to whom life's just a game.
A washerwoman's only child . . .
His days are spent in running wild.
Abanazer (*with cunning*) A wild one, eh? (*He chuckles*) *I'll* soon tame him.
Take me to this place in the twinkling of an eye . . .
For the Lamp *shall* be mine . . . then the boy will *die.*
(*He laughs harshly*)
Slave To China, then. Our journey we'll begin.
I'll set you down where he's sure to be,
In the market place of Old Peking.

There is an instant Black-out. Both exit under cover of the darkness

SCENE 1

Old Peking

A Chinese market place with quaint stalls and houses surrounding it. Widow Twankey's laundry is up R, *and has a practical door*

When the scene begins, it is daylight and the Citizens of Peking are singing and dancing happily

Song 1 (*Choristers*)

At the end of the song, Aladdin enters jauntily up L, *and moves down* C

Aladdin (*brightly*) Hi, gang.

All greet him cheerily

What's all the excitement?
Girl Weren't you watching TV-am this morning, Aladdin? The Princess Badroulbador's coming through the streets today with her father . . . on their way to the Imperial Baths.
Boy Which means . . . she'll be passing through this very market place.
Aladdin Princess Badroulbador? Ohhhhhh. She's the most beautiful girl in the whole of China.
Girl How do *you* know? No-one's ever seen her face.
Aladdin *I* have. I climbed the walls of the Imperial Palace gardens only last week and watched her feeding the peacocks.
Boy (*aghast*) But Aladdin . . . you know what the *penalty* is for looking at the Princess's face. Instant execution.
Aladdin (*laughing*) So what? They'll have to catch me first. Besides . . . what good is it having a beautiful Princess if no-one's allowed to look at her? It's a criminal waste. (*He glances round*) Now where's the best spot for me to catch a glimpse of her when she arrives here?
Girl (*horrified*) You don't mean you're going to try and see her *again*?

Aladdin Why not? I might even ask her to *marry* me if I can get close enough.

All laugh

What's so funny?

Boy Marry *you*? Why, she won't even *notice* you. You're nothing but the son of a poor old washerwoman.

Aladdin I know ... but I can dream, can't I? Besides ... I've got a funny feeling my fortunes are going to change, so she'd better snap me up now whilst she's still got the chance. After all ... when I'm rich and famous, I'll be able to marry any girl I please.

Girl Yes ... but what if you *don't* please any of them?

All laugh

Aladdin (*smiling*) Well ... I'll worry about that when the time comes. Just for now, I'm so happy I could burst ... and when I'm feeling like this, there's absolutely nothing in the world that's going to depress me.

Song 2 (*Aladdin*)

At the end of the song, the Chorus exit cheerily

Aladdin makes to exit into the laundry, but before he can do so, there is a great cry of distress from inside

Widow Twankey comes staggering out, clutching at her bosom as though in pain

(*Startled*) Mother ... (*He hurries to her*)

Twankey (*gasping*) Help. Police. Murder.

Aladdin (*very concerned*) Mother. What on earth's the matter?

Twankey (*clutching at him*) I've been swindled. Swindled. Some woman's just paid for her laundry with a dud coin.

Aladdin Counterfeit?

Twankey Yes. She had two. (*She wails*) Oh, whatever are we going to do? I haven't made enough money to pay the rent, and we haven't a thing in the house to eat.

Aladdin (*uncomfortable*) Oh ... well ... you ... er ... you don't have to worry about food for *me*, Mum. As a matter of fact, I've already eaten.

Twankey (*startled*) Eh?

Aladdin I found a hundred yen note in the street, so I had lunch down at the harbour.

Twankey (*annoyed*) Do you mean to tell me that I've been starving to death at home while you've been stuffing your face inside one of these floating restaurants?

Aladdin (*contrite*) I'm afraid so, Mum. I had oysters on one junk, and king prawns on another. Fried octopus on a third, and on the biggest junk of all, I had egg fried rice, bamboo shoots, sweet and sour pork and chicken chop suey.

Twankey (*wincing*) Ooooh. I don't know how you can keep it all down.

Aladdin (*uneasily*) I'm not sure that I can. To tell you the truth ... I'm starting to feel a little bit sick. (*He holds his stomach*)

Twankey (*triumphantly*) Yes ... and it jolly well serves you right. I've warned you before about eating too much junk food. Anyway ... I'll soon take your mind off it. You can come and give me a hand in the laundry. I need someone to wind the mangle.

Aladdin (*dismayed*) Oh, Mum ... Do I *have* to?

Twankey (*fiercely*) Yes, you do. It's about time you stopped running round the streets enjoying yourself, and did some work for a change. You're so lazy, you don't even walk in your sleep, now. You hitch-hike. Ooooh, if your poor father were still alive to see the way you behave now that he's dead, he'd climb out of his coffin and die of shame.

Aladdin Oh, don't get upset with me, Mum. I know I should do more to help you. It's just that I want to enjoy life whilst I'm still young enough to do it. But don't worry. I'll make you proud of me one day, I promise. Just you wait and see.

Twankey (*resignedly*) Yes ... you sound just like your father. "Don't worry, Titania," he'd say to me. "One of these days, Dame Fortune's going to come knocking at that laundry door." (*She snorts in derision*) Dame Fortune. The only one who ever came knocking was her *daughter*, Miss Fortune.

Aladdin (*curiously*) You know ... speaking of Father ... I've often wondered about him. I mean ... it's such a long time ago since he died, I can hardly remember what he looked like. For instance ... I've got such (*he gives his own hair colour*) hair, and you've got such (*he gives Twankey's hair colour*) hair ... well ... what colour hair did *he* have?

Twankey I've no idea. He didn't have time to take his hat off.

Aladdin (*smiling*) Well, then ... How did you come to meet him?

Twankey Oh, I can remember *that*. Covered with perspiration and sweat, he was. He'd just done one thousand metres in five seconds flat.

Aladdin (*incredulous*) But that's impossible.

Twankey No it isn't. He'd just fallen down a lift-shaft. (*She beams*) Still ... it was love at first fright. There he was ... six feet tall, chest as hairy as a busted sofa, and one beautiful blue glass eye.

Aladdin (*startled*) Glass eye??

Twankey (*quickly*) Oh, I didn't realize it at first. It just came out during the conversation. Anyway ... to cut a long story short ... he took me for a gin and tonic and Schwepped me off me feet. (*She sighs happily*) Oh, those were the days. Fifteen years we were married and not once did we think of divorce. Murder, yes ... but not divorce. Poor Cuthbert. I still miss him, you know. He was a model husband.

Aladdin (*surprised*) Really?

Twankey (*nodding*) Not a *working* model, mind you, but I could hardly blame him for that. He was very superstitious, you see. Daren't work any week that had a Wednesday in it. (*Fondly*) But I didn't mind. You see ... in spite of everything ... he'd have *died* for me, that man would. He told me so, many a time. "Titania," he'd say, "I'll swing for you yet." (*She heaves a sigh of resignation*) And now he's gone. And here *I* am ... a poor, helpless little widow woman with a wayward son and a great big pile of other people's dirty washing to attend to. Oh, whatever's to become of us?

Aladdin (*brightly*) Cheer up, Mum. Let's go in and have a nice cup of tea, then I'll give you a hand to sort it all out.

Twankey (*cheering up*) Will you? Oh, thank you, son. You're not a bad boy at heart, are you? I'll put the kettle on.

They exit into the laundry

As they do so, the Lights dim and Abanazar enters up L, *a green spotlight on him*

Abanazer (*glancing around*) So this is Peking ... and here I am in the market place. But where is the boy Aladdin? He who will help me find the Magic Lamp. I must meet him ... and soon. For then, and only then, may I discover the hidden entrance to that mystic cave and fulfil my destiny. (*He glances round again*) I'll explore yonder side-street.

He exits R, *and the Lights come up again*

A great commotion is heard off up L, *and a crowd of laughing girls scatter on to the stage, pursued by the blindfolded figure of Wishee Washee who is trying to catch one of them. They call to him in teasing tones*

Girls Here, Wishee. This way, Wishee. Behind you ... *etc.*

As he blunders around, two girls quickly exit to return with an old swabbing mop and a large wet sponge, respectively. The girl holding the mop holds it out in front of Wishee's fingers and he clutches at it

Wishee (*triumphantly*) Aha ... I've caught somebody by the hair. Oooh, I bet *you* don't use Silvikrin. Come on, now. You told me I'd get a big juicy kiss if I caught one of you. Where is it? (*He puckers his lips*)

Girl Here it is.

Wishee lets go of the mop-head, and the girl with the sponge quickly squashes it into his face

As he reacts, the girls shriek with laughter and quickly exit

Wishee (*pulling off the blindfold and calling after them*) You rotten, horrible lot. That's the last time I play Blind Man's Buff with *you*. (*He winces*) Oooh, I'm all wet. (*He dabs at himself with the blindfold and suddenly notices the audience*) Oh ... hello. (*He peers at them closely*) Oooooh. Here ... you're not tonight's audience, are you? (*Coaxingly*) Come on ... speak to Wishee. Are you tonight's audience?

Audience reaction

Oooooooooooh. (*He titters*) Don't you look funny? (*Remembering himself*) No, no. Don't get upset. I'm not trying to be rude. Honest. It's just that we've never had an audience like *you* in to watch us, before. I mean ... your faces. They're all *white* ... and your eyes are the wrong shape. You don't look like Chinese at all. (*Quickly*) But don't worry about it. As long as you can understand Chinese, you'll have a smashing time with us. You ... er ... you *do* understand Chinese, don't you?

Audience reaction

Of course you do. (*He indicates a little girl near the front*) This little girl down here does ... (*to her*) ... don't you, love? No? *No??* But you *must* do. Whereabouts do you live?

The child names the district

Where?? (*He repeats the district the child gives*) Well ... everybody speaks Chinese *there*. Every time the rent man comes round for his money and knocks on the door, the kids run out and shout "Shint in. Shint in." (*He chortles*) Anyway ... now I know we can all understand each other, I'd better introduce myself. My name's Wishee Washee, and I'm world-famous in our street. I am. I've only got to put me head outside the door and everybody shouts "Hiya, Wishee". (*Thoughtfully*) Mind you ... I'm not living at home right now ... and I've never been in this part of the city before so I haven't got pals to talk to me. Here ... I'll tell you what, though ... how about *you* being my pals? Every time I come on, I'll shout "Hiya, kids" and you can shout back "Hiya, Wishee" and then I won't feel so lonely. Will you do that?

Audience reaction

Let's have a little practice then.

He practises with the audience until he is satisfied with the response

Right. Smashing. Now then ... I suppose you're all wondering what I'm doing here, aren't you? As a matter of fact, I'm looking for a new job. I lost me old one because of illness. The boss got sick of me. No, but I'll do anything ... as long as it's honest. I've had lots of different jobs, you know. Once I was a liver, brain and lung specialist. I *was*. I was a butcher. I had to give it up, though. It was an offal job. But then ... then ... I went right to the top of the ladder in television. Oh, yes. I was one of the high-ups. I fixed aerials on rooftops. Anyway ... if you hear of any jobs going, you won't forget to let me know, will you? All right then. See you later.

With a cheery wave, Wishee exits down R

As he does so, Widow Twankey enters from the laundry carrying a large notice on which is printed "Asist" "Assyst" "Asyst", all crossed through, and "Help wanted" substituted

Twankey (*to the audience*) Oh, I say, boys and girls. I've had a smashing idea. I'm going to hang this notice up and see if I can get somebody to help me in the laundry. (*She hangs it on the doorframe*)

Abanazar enters behind her

Abanazar Aha. I'll see if *this* old hag knows where the boy lives. (*Loudly*) Good-morning, madam.
Twankey (*turning, startled*) Oh ... it's (*she names a well-known personality*) (*Concerned*) Here ... I'm sorry you've hurt your head. (*She indicates his turban*)

Abanazar (*forcing a smile*) Very droll, madam. Very droll. (*With vigour*) Tell me . . . are you Peking's oldest inhabitant?

Twankey (*indignant*) Certainly not. I've only just arrived at the age of thirty-two.

Abanazar (*eyeing her askance*) Really? (*Aside*) I wonder what delayed her?

Twankey Here . . . I don't remonstrate notifying *you* around these parts before.

Abanazar Hardly surprising, madam. I happen to be a stranger.

Twankey (*pleased*) I *thought* as much. The second I set eyes on that nose of yours, I said to myself "That fellow would make a perfect stranger".

Abanazar (*puzzled*) Nose??? (*He feels his nose*)

Twankey Oh, yes. There's not many people in this part of the world with nostrils like a two-door garage. Where do you come from?

Abanazar (*proudly*) Egypt, madam, is the land of my birth.

Twankey (*kindly*) Never mind, love. Terrible things happen in other countries, as well. (*Eagerly*) Here . . . you're not married, are you?

Abanazar (*irritated*) No.

Twankey Oh . . . single. (*She preens herself*)

Abanazar Certainly not.

Twankey (*frowning*) You're not married and you're not single? Well what are you?

Abanazar (*impatiently*) If you must know . . . I'm a grass widower.

Twankey (*delightedly*) Ooh, how lucky we met. I'm a vegetarian. (*She pushes him playfully and sends him flying*) Here . . . I'm also a widow . . . with one little boy.

Abanazar (*uninterested*) Really?

Twankey Mind you . . . I'm a bit worried about him. He hasn't had a job since he left school, and he keeps coming home covered with gold paint.

Abanazar Gold paint???

Twankey Yes. I think he's developed a gilt complex. (*She chortles*) Oh, poor Aladdin. I do make fun of him.

Abanazar (*startled*) Aladdin? Did you say *Aladdin*?

Twanky (*proudly*) That's right. Aladdin Hydrangeas Twankey. (*Confidentially*) We called him Aladdin after his grandfather.

Abanazar But what about the Hydrangeas?

Twankey Lost, two nil. (*She giggles*)

Abanazar (*aside*) Can this be the boy I'm looking for? No, no. It's impossible. And yet . . . Perhaps I'd better make further enquiries. (*To Twankey*) This . . . er . . . son of yours, madam. Is he a rather *remarkable* person?

Twankey What? I'll say he's remarkable. Do you know . . . that boy was *walking* before he was six weeks old. The bottom fell out of his pram.

Abanazar (*after a wince*) But tell me . . . he is brave, honest and intelligent?

Twankey Of course he is. There hasn't been a boy like him in our family for hundreds of years.

Abanazar Ah . . . so you have a large family tree?

Twankey (*puzzled*) No. We haven't even got a plant-pot. (*She indicates* *upstage to the laundry*) There's not much soil round these houses ... (*She babbles on as Abanazar speaks*)

Abanazar (*eyes glittering excitedly*) It must be him. It must. (*Delightedly*) Found ... the very boy I've been looking for. (*To Twankey, loudly*) May I meet this little *angel?*

Twankey (*turning back to him*) Eh? Oh ... yes. Yes, of course you can. He's inside the laundry boiling an egg for me. I'll give him a shout. (*She calls*) Aladdin ...

Aladdin enters from the laundry holding his nose

Aladdin Oh, Mum ... that egg was *rotten*.

Twankey Don't blame me. I only laid the table. Come over here and say hello to this feller in the polo-necked sweater.

Abanazar (*puzzled*) Eh? (*He looks down at himself*)

Twankey (*realizing*) Oh ... silly old me. It's not a polo-necked sweater at all. It's his bottom lip. (*To Aladdin*) Say something nice to him. He might slip us a few yen if we're lucky.

Aladdin (*to Abanazar*) Good-morning, sir.

Abanazar (*beaming*) My dear boy. You're the very *image* of him.

Aladdin and Twankey look puzzled

Tell me ... did you never hear your father speak of his long-lost brother?

Aladdin (*surprised*) No, sir. Never.

Abanazar (*flinging his arms wide*) Then behold. I am the long-lost brother he never spoke about.

Aladdin and Twankey react

Embrace me, Nephew. (*He hugs Aladdin*)

Twankey (*quickly recovering*) Here, here. Take your measly, mucky maulers off him. You don't know where he's been.

Aladdin breaks free

It's all right you coming here and claiming to be my late husband's long-washed brother, but can you *prove* it? Can you identifying yourself?

Abanazar But of course ... Do you have such a thing as a small mirror about your person?

Twankey (*puzzled*) Mirror? (*She gets a small mirror from her apron pocket and extends it to him*) Like this, you mean?

Abanazar Exactly. (*He takes it*) Now ... you wish me to identify myself? (*He looks into the mirror*) Yes. That's me, all right. What further proof could be needed? (*He hands it back to her*)

Twankey (*doubtfully*) Well ... I don't know. (*To the audience*) There's something about him I don't trust, boys and girls. Do *you* think he's telling the truth?

Audience reaction

Abanazar (*shrugging*) Oh, well ... If you wish to take notice of *that* spotty-faced, sweet-sucking pack of dim-witted dunderheads and disown your millionaire brother-in-law, I'll be off. (*He turns as though to exit*)

Twankey Millionaire??? (*Quickly*) Oh. Here, wait a minute. I've just remembered something.

Abanazar (*aside with a smirk*) I thought she might do. (*He turns back to her*)

Twankey Of *course* we remember him never talking about you. He hardly ever stopped, did he, Aladdin? Er . . . *what* was it he called you?

Abanazar (*beaming*) Why, Abanazar, dear sister-in-law. Abanazar.

Twankey Yes . . . that's what it was. Abanazar. Here . . . but we can't keep calling you that now you're one of the family, can we? Course we can't. We'll call you Ab, for short.

Abanazar (*incredulously*) Ab??

Twankey Why not? I mean . . . (*She indicates Aladdin*) He's Aladdin, so you can call him Al for short. And I'm Titania . . . so you can call me . . . any time you feel like it. (*She pushes him playfully and sends him flying*)

Aladdin (*in a daze*) A long-lost uncle *and* a millionaire. I must be dreaming.

Twankey Well if you are, don't bother waking up. (*To Abanazar*) Here . . . Abbi . . . You wouldn't happen to have a few thousand yen to spare till I can get to the Post Office and draw me widow's pension, would you?

Abanazar (*with mock regret*) Alas . . . for the moment my purse is as empty as a politician's promise. But soon . . . very soon . . . you shall have riches beyond the dreams of avarice. I, Abanazar, do swear it.

Twankey (*to the audience*) Oooh, did you hear that, boys and girls? We're going to have riches beyond the dreams of Aberystwyth. (*She almost faints with joy*)

Aladdin (*frowning*) Just a minute, Uncle. If you're *really* a millionaire, why are you walking around in *those* old rags? Where are your fine clothes? And jewels?

Abanazar (*aside*) Curses. The boy is sharper than I thought. I must allay his suspicions. (*To Aladdin*) The answer is simple, dear Nephew . . . I dress like this to escape the attentions of those who would rob wealthy merchants such as myself.

Twankey (*nodding*) Oh, yes. He's quite right, Aladdin. There's all sorts of funny people running round the streets these days. Only this morning I was walking down (*she names a local street*) when somebody tried to rob *me*. "Hand over your money," he said.

Aladdin (*shocked*) Mum . . .

Twankey "Money?" I said. "Money? *I* haven't got any money." But he wouldn't believe me. "All right, then," he said. "If you won't hand it over, I shall have to *search* you." Oh, girls . . . he searched me *all over*. I think he must have been a sailor, because he definitely had submarine hands . . . I didn't know where they were going to pop up next. Anyway . . . he didn't find anything . . . but I'd enjoyed myself so much, I wrote him out a cheque for his trouble.

Abanazar (*firmly*) As I was saying . . . Very soon, undreamed of wealth shall be yours, for a few miles away, my great treasure store lies hidden . . . secreted in a vast cavern containing more jewels than the desert has grains of sand.

Aladdin (*impressed*) Gosh. How soon can we get there?
Abanazar (*leering*) Patience, dear Nephew, patience. I'll take you there
when the time is right . . . perhaps tomorrow. Perhaps *tonight*. I'll make
preparations and . . . never fear . . . return to collect you.
Aladdin (*eagerly*) I'll be here.

Abanazar exits with an evil chuckle

(*To Twankey*) Oh, Mum. Our worries are over. We're going to have so
much money you'll be able to sell the laundry lease and live in luxury for
the rest of your life.
Twankey (*excitedly*) Ooh, I can hardly wait. Come on. Let's go in and start
making lists of everything we'll want to buy.

*They exit into the laundry chatting eagerly. As they exit, a loud voice is
heard off up* L

Vizier (*off*) Make way for the Emperor. Make way for the Emperor.

*With much excitement, the market place is filled with Citizens, all agog to
see their ruler. With great pomp the Grand Vizier enters up* L, *flanked by
two fierce looking Guards*

His most Celestial Highness, Chee Kin Chow Mein . . . Emperor of
China. (*He indicates off up* L)

*A loud discordant fanfare sounds and four massive Slaves enter supporting
an ornate sedan chair. They move down* C *and it can be seen that there is no
bottom to the sedan and the Emperor is in fact walking along inside it. The
chair is lowered, and his head appears over the top. With much floundering,
muttering and struggles, the drapes are forced aside, and the doddery old
Emperor appears*

All kow-tow and hiss loudly

Emperor (*peering around*) Is this it, Vizier? Have we arrived?
Vizier (*moving down to join the Emperor*) Indeed we have, Your Highness.
The Imperial Baths are yonder. (*He indicates off down* R)
Emperor (*nodding*) Good. Good. And where's me daughter, the Princess
Badroulbador?
Vizier (*glancing off up* L) Arriving now, Your Highness . . . and suitably
veiled.
Emperor (*nodding*) Splendid, splendid. Well . . . get on with it, man. Read
them the usual proclamation.
Vizier (*unrolling a small scroll and reading*) "By order of His Most Celestial
Highness . . . Lord of the Moon and Master of the Sun. Divine Prince of
Peking, Shantung, Kwangtung, Lambstung, Hong Kong, King Kong and
Ping Pong——"
Emperor (*testily*) Oh, never mind the commercials . . . get on with the nitty-
gritty.
Vizier "No man shall gaze upon the face of his most beautiful daughter,
Princess Badroulbador unless they wish to die. Therefore . . . to prevent

unfortunate 'accidents' . . . you are commanded to return to your homes and shutter your windows until the Royal Visit is over." (*He re-rolls the scroll*)

With due deference, the Citizens quickly withdraw

Emperor (*beaming*) Now then . . . summon me daughter then buzz off and blow up me water wings. (*He rubs his hands in glee*) Oooh, I can hardly wait to get me shoes and socks off.

The Vizier signals off up L, *then exits down* R, *followed by the sedan chair and bearers*

Princess Badroulbador and Handmaidens enter. The Princess is veiled

(*Greeting her*) Come along, Badroulbador. Here we are at the Imperial Baths. Just think. This may be the very last time we have to use these public baths for our yearly bathe. If all goes well, the rich Prince Pekoe will ask for your hand in marriage and we'll be able to build a pool of our own in the Royal Palace. (*He chuckles*)

Princess (*protesting*) But I don't want to marry Prince Pekoe, Father. He's old and fat and as ugly as sin.

Emperor (*thoughtfully*) Yes . . . I have to admit he's no oil painting. When his grandfather was born, everyone passed out cigars. When his father was born, everyone passed out cigarettes. But when *he* was born, everybody just passed out. (*Resolutely*) Still . . . looks aren't everything. He's very rich and that's all that matters. You know we're almost penniless, and unless you marry someone *wealthy*, the whole country will go bankrupt. So come along. Into the Bath House and prepare yourself.

Princess (*pleading*) Oh, Father . . . please don't make me marry him. Please.

Emperor (*annoyed*) Now that is enough, Badroulbador. You're in a very disagreeable mood this morning and I won't have it. Out of the kindness of my heart I've allowed you to leave the palace and come with me, but if this is the way you're going to reward me, I shall go into the baths alone. You will remain here in the market place until you come to your senses.

He snaps his fan angrily and totters off down R

The Princess bursts into tears and covers her face with her hands. Anxiously, her Handmaidens surround her

So-Shy Don't cry, Princess. I'm sure your father would not be so cruel as to *force* you into marriage. (*She hands the Princess a silk kerchief*)

Princess (*unveiling to wipe her eyes*) Oh, So-Shy . . . if only that were true.

Aladdin enters from the laundry, un-noticed

Aladdin (*startled*) The Princess. (*He draws back*) How beautiful she is . . . even though she's crying. I wonder what's wrong? (*He hesitates*) It's no use. I've simply got to *meet* her. (*He crosses to the group and taps the Princess on the shoulder*) Hello.

Princess (*turning, startled*) A boy . . .

The Handmaidens react in horror

Aladdin A *man.*

So-Shy (*trying to come between them*) Oh, please. Please go away. If you're discovered looking at her, you'll be killed on the spot.

Aladdin I don't care. I'll defy death itself merely to gaze upon her beauty.

Princess (*wonderingly*) Do you *really* mean that?

Aladdin But of course, Princess. You're the most beautiful lady in all China.

So-Shy Who *are* you?

Aladdin Aladdin Twankey. Only son of a humble washerwoman.

Princess (*to So-Shy*) Oh, So-Shy ... how handsome he is. If only he were rich.

So-Shy (*anxiously*) Princess. Your veil.

Remembering, the Princess quickly begins to cover her face

Aladdin (*quickly*) Oh, please ... there's no need to do that.

Princess (*pausing*) But there *is*, Aladdin. If anyone should see us together ...

Aladdin Let them. I'd risk anything just to look into your eyes. I love you, Princess.

The Handmaidens react in confusion

Princess Oh, Aladdin. You don't know how often I've longed for someone to say those words to me. But don't you understand? Love for us is impossible, so you must promise never to say such a thing again.

Aladdin If you insist, Princess. But remember ... true lovers need no words spoken. They can hear them in their hearts.

Song 3 (*Aladdin and Princess*)

At the end of the song, they move down L, *in deep conversation leaving the worried-looking Handmaidens and So-Shy up* R

Wishee Washee enters DR

Wishee Hiya, kids. (*He sees the notice on the laundry door*) Hey ... just what I'm looking for. Oh, wait a minute thought. I don't want to work for anyone nasty, do I? I'd better find out what the owner's like before I go in. (*He sees Aladdin and the Princess*) These two might know. (*He crosses to Aladdin and taps him on the shoulder*) 'Scuse me.

Aladdin (*turning*) Yes? (*Recognizing him*) Wishee.

Wishee (*surprised*) Aladdin. My old mate.

Aladdin What are *you* doing in this part of the city?

Wishee I'm looking for a job and I saw that notice on the laundry door and ... (*He notices the Princess*) Oh, hello ...

The Princess quickly fixes her veil in position and turns away

(*To Aladdin*) A bit shy, is she?

Aladdin (*laughing*) Of course not. It's just that no-one's supposed to look at her face under pain of death. This is the Princess Badroulbador.

Wishee Princess Black-droopy-drawers? Oh. (*To the Princess*) Pleased to meet you. (*He realizes*) Princess?? (*He panics*) Oooer. Quick, Aladdin. Make a dash for it. Scarper. Run for your life.

Aladdin (*puzzled*) Why?

Wishee (*amazed*) Why? Why? Didn't you just say that nobody had to look at her face under pain of death?

The Princess moves away and up to her Handmaidens

Well *you've* done it. You've parked your peepers on her. If anyone finds out you could lose your head.

Aladdin Who cares? I've already lost my heart.

Wishee Yes . . . it's all right for you. But what about me? I've looked at her, too.

Aladdin Don't worry, Wishee. You save yourself. I'm going to stay here and talk with her even if it costs me my life.

With a smile, Aladdin crosses to the Princess and her Handmaidens. Wishee glances worriedly down R, and groans

Wishee (*to himself*) I think it's going to. Here comes the Emperor. (*He closes his eyes in anguish*)

The Emperor enters in an old-fashioned bathing costume, water wings, frogman's flippers and carrying a loofah

Emperor (*muttering in an annoyed fashion*) Can't find me rubber duck anywhere. (*Looking towards the group*) Badroulbador? Have you seen my . . .?

Aladdin and the others turn quickly to face him in dismay

(*Outraged*) What?? He's talking to the Princess. He's *talking* to her. (*He yells loudly*) Guards. Guards. Off with his head.

There is great confusion. Citizens, Guards, Policemen and the Vizier quickly fill the stage

Aladdin is seized by the Guards

Wishee (*to the Emperor*) Oh, Your Royal Emptiness. He didn't *mean* to look at her. Don't chop his head off. Just give him a short back and sides.

Emperor (*indignant*) Certainly not. Wouldn't suit him at all. Send for the Executioner.

Widow Twankey enters from the laundry

Twankey What's happening? What's going on?

Emperor Nothing at all, madam. (*He indicates Aladdin*) It's his head that's coming off.

Twankey (*aghast*) What? My Aladdin? Oh, no. No. You can't chop his head off.

Emperor And why not??? I am the all-powerful one and my least wish must be obeyed. Everyone must do as I say.

Wishee Blimey. He thinks he's (*he names an unpopular politician or Trade Union leader*).

Emperor Bah. I'm more powerful than him. I have only to breathe out and hundreds of Chinese can die.

Twankey I'm not surprised. Your breath smells terrible. (*She fans herself with her hand*)

Emperor (*enraged*) Aaaaaagh. Where's that Executioner? Telephone him at once.

Wishee Oh, we can't do that, Your Royal Distemperer. He's just been cut off.

Emperor Bah. Hand me a sword, Vizier. I'll chop his head off *myself.*

Princess (*coming forward*) No, Father. Please.

Emperor Silence when you speak to me. (*To Aladdin*) Prisoner, kneel.

Aladdin is forced to his knees

Twankey Oh . . . he's going to commit chop-suicide. Mercy. Mercy. (*She flings herself at the Emperor's feet*)

A sword is passed to the Emperor by the Vizier. The Emperor ignores Twankey and turns to Aladdin, raising the sword

Wishee (*thinking quickly*) Ooo-er. Wait. Wait, Your Royal Whatsit. You'll never cut his head off like that. You're standing at the wrong angle.

Emperor (*unsure*) I am?

Wishee Of course you are. You'll have to move back a bit.

The Emperor moves back a step

A bit more.

The Emperor moves back another step

Bit more still.

The Emperor moves another step back and topples over Twankey's body with a yell of surprise. The crowd react

Quick, Aladdin. Run for it.

Aladdin springs free as everyone attempts to help the Emperor untangle himself

Aladdin (*càlling*) Thanks, Wishee.

He dashes off down L, *to the delight of the Princess*

Vizier (*noticing*) After him.

Police and Guards rush after Aladdin

The rest struggle in confusion and the scene ends in a quick fade to a Black-out

SCENE 2

A quiet street

Abanazer enters, rubbing his hands with glee

Abanazar At last, at last. The Magic Lamp is almost within my grasp. That
fool Aladdin will hand it over without a second thought . . . and then . . .
then . . . (*He laughs harshly*) Master of the Universe I shall be. (*He scowls*)
But wait . . . Now I must discover exactly where this mysterious cavern
lies. (*He rubs the ring*)

There is a flash and the Slave appears

Slave You summoned me, O master?
Abanazar (*snarling*) Of course I summoned you, you dim-witted djinn. I
need further information. The boy Aladdin is found and within my power.
Now tell me the way to the cavern of the Lamp.
Slave   North of the City, and East of the sea . . .
            Where the sky meets the mountains, tonight you must be.
            Then the stars in the heavens will show you the way
            To that long hidden cavern. O master . . . good-day.

He bows and exits

Abanazar (*triumphant*) Tonight. Tonight. (*Singing*) I'll have my Lamp
tonight . . . I'll hold it and the world will be mine . . . (*He remembers
himself*) Ahem . . . I must work quickly. I'll collect the boy and we'll leave
for the mountains at once.

He exits L

As he does so, Widow Twankey enters R. *She carries a large jug of water
and a very big metal or plastic funnel. (See Production Note on page v for
this next sequence)*

Twankey Hello, boys and girls. Oh, what a day it's been, hasn't it? First of
all they tried to chop off my poor Aladdin's head, and now they've sent
the bailiff round to throw me out of my laundry unless I pay the rent. Still,
not to worry, because I've had a marvellous idea. I've thought of a
smashing way to raise the money just by using this jug of water, this old
funnel and a two-penny piece. As soon as somebody stupid comes along,
I'll show you how it's done. (*She glances off*) Oh . . . here comes that
Grand Vizier fellow. He'll be just perfect. Watch me stop him in his tracks
with this seductive pose. (*She puts the jug of water behind her and strikes a
pose*)

The Vizier enters L

Vizier (*startled*) Good heavens . . . what a terrible accident. (*Realizing*) Oh
. . . Widow Twankey. It's you.
Twankey (*sweetly*) Well, well, well. Fancy meeting you again. You . . . er . . .
you wouldn't be interested in making a bit of money, would you?

Vizier Money? (*His eyes lighting up*) Why . . . er . . . yes. Of course I would. What do I have to do?

Twankey (*beaming*) Well . . . I know a trick with a two-penny piece and this funnel . . . and I'll bet you a pound note that you can't do the same trick.

Vizier (*smirking*) Utter nonsense.

Twankey Will you bet me, then?

Vizier Certainly. Here's my pound note. (*He puts down a pound note*)

Twankey And here's mine. (*She puts a pound note down*) Now then . . . stick this funnel spout down the front of your trousers . . .

The Vizier looks puzzled but does so

(*Producing the 2p*) now tilt your head back and balance this coin in the middle of your forehead. (*She gives him the coin*) All you have to do is straighten up when I give the word, and catch that coin in the top of that funnel without using your hands.

Vizier Catch the coin. Simple. (*He begins to prepare himself*)

Twankey Oh . . . there's just one more thing. If you make a noise while you're doing it . . . you lose the money. All right?

Vizier Right. (*He tips his head back, places the coin in position and waits for the command*)

Twankey Are you ready? (*She picks up the jug of water*) Allez-oops. (*She tips the water into the funnel top with a grin*)

Vizier (*straightening up sharply*) Aaaaaaaaah.

Twankey (*beaming*) You lose.

She puts down the jug, snatches up the notes and exits quickly L

Vizier (*gingerly mopping at this "wet" trouser front*) The flea-bitten old harridan. I'm soaking. Bah. I've been diddled. (*He glances off* R) Just a minute. Here comes that idiot Wishee Washee. I'll see if I can get my money back from *him*. (*He puts the jug behind him*)

Wishee enters R

Wishee (*as he enters*) Hiya, kids.

Vizier Well, well, well. Fancy meeting you again. You . . . er . . . you wouldn't be interested in making a bit of money, would you?

Wishee Money? (*His eyes lighting up*) Oh, yes, Mr Vizier. I'm always interested in making a bit of money.

Vizier (*delightedly*) Good, good. Well——

Wishee I've never had much money, you see.

Vizier Really? Well, now's your chance to make some. I know a trick——

Wishee I come from a very poor family, you see. In fact we were so poor, my mother had to put two babies in one nappy. It was the only way she could make ends meet.

Vizier Er . . . how interesting. Now about this money. I know a——

Wishee (*starting to sniffle*) Even my little sister had to be made in Japan.

Vizier (*impatiently*) But surely your *father* did some work?

Wishee Well of course he did. He was a fisherman. But he was poor as well.

The only thing *he* could afford to do was to take us all swimming when he went out in his fishing boat. He was ever such a good teacher.

Vizier (*uninterested*) Really?

Wishee Mind you ... it used to take us ages to get out of the sacks.

Vizier (*defeated*) Bah. (*He turns to exit*)

Wishee Here ... don't go. I thought you were going to tell me how to make some money?

Vizier (*returning*) Very well, then. (*He forces a smile*) Now I know a trick with a two-penny piece and this funnel ... and I'll bet you a pound note that you can't do the same trick.

Wishee Oooh. I bet you I can. Just let me get my pound note out. (*He gets one*)

Vizier Place it down there ... (*He indicates*) ... and here's mine. (*He puts his note down*)

Wishee Now then. What do I have to do?

Vizier (*beaming*) Stick the spout of this funnel down the top of your trousers like so ... (*He thrusts the funnel top into Wishee's waistband*)

Wishee (*his face contorting*) Oooooooooooh. (*To the audience*) It isn't half cold.

Vizier Now tilt your head back and balance this coin in the middle of your forehead ... (*He gives him the coin*) All you have to do is to straighten up when I give the word, and catch the coin in the top of the funnel without using your hands.

Wishee (*beaming*) I can do that easily.

Vizier Just one more thing. If you make a noise while you're doing it ... you lose the money. All right?

Wishee Right. (*He tilts his head back and places the coin in position*)

Vizier (*picking up the jug*) Are you ready? Allez-oops. (*He tips the water into the funnel*)

Wishee (*straightening with a yell*) Oooooooooooh.

Vizier (*smirking*) You lose.

He puts down the jug, snatches up the money and exits quickly R

Wishee (*mopping at himself*) Ooh, the rotten old thing, I'm soaking and he's diddled me out of half my unemployment money. I'll have to get it back somehow. (*He looks off* L) Oh ... here comes the Emperor. I'll see if I can get it off him. (*He puts the jug behind him*)

The Emperor enters

Well, well, well. Fancy meeting you again. Your Sequestrial Distemperer. You ... er ... you wouldn't be interested in making a bit of money, would you?

Emperor Money? (*His eyes lighting up*) Why, yes, of course I would. How do I do it?

The trick is repeated on the Emperor and Wishee goes off with the money, leaving the Emperor soaking and angry

Bah. Fiddle-de-dee and sagger-makers bottom knockers. I'm soaking.

(*He fumes*) I've got to get that money back somehow. (*He glances off*) Aha . . . here comes Widow Twankey. I'll play the same trick on her.

Widow Twankey enters

Well, well, well. Fancy meeting you again. You . . . er . . . you wouldn't be interested in making a bit of money, would you?

Twankey (*giving the audience a "look"*) I think I've just heard an echo. (*To the Emperor*) Why . . . of course I'd be interested, Your Magneticals. What do I have to do? (*She beams at him*)

Emperor He he he.

The trick is repeated with Widow Twankey up to the point where the water is poured into the funnel. There is no reaction from Twankey

(*Trying again*) Allez-oops. (*He pours more water*)

Still no reaction. Puzzled, the Emperor pulls out the funnel from the top of her skirt and peers down it. Seeing no obstruction, he replaces it and pours again. Still no reaction from Twankey, but when he finishes pouring, she straightens and the coin drops into the top of the funnel. Beaming she removes the funnel and picks up the money)

I don't understand it? (*He looks into the jug*) What happened to all the water?

Twankey (*moving away from him*) Oh, that. (*She produces a hot-water bottle from inside her waistband*) It all went into *this*. Bye-bye.

The Emperor reacts and chases her off in a temper

Black-out

SCENE 3

The gardens of the Imperial Palace

An attractive Chinese garden with a small, open pavilion up C. *The Princess is standing outside the pavilion with So-Shy. Other Handmaidens are dotted around the garden chatting quietly*

Princess (*anxiously*) Oh, So-Shy . . . I do hope Aladdin managed to escape from my father's guards.

So-Shy Don't worry, Your Highness. If the tales *I've* been hearing about him are true, they wouldn't stand a chance of catching him.

Princess Are you sure? (*She turns away restlessly*) Oh, if only I knew for certain.

So-Shy Forgive me for saying so, Your Highness . . . but you seem very concerned about him. I know he was handsome and charming, but he's only the son of a washerwoman, and can mean nothing to a royal Princess like you.

Princess (*turning to her quickly*) How wrong you are, So-Shy. He means everything to me. You see . . . I think I've fallen in love with him.

Everyone looks shocked

So-Shy But what about Prince Pekoe, Your Highness? The man you're expected to marry. Even now he's approaching the Imperial Palace with his caravan of great riches.

Princess I don't care. He can keep his riches. If I can't marry Aladdin, I'll die an old maid. You see, So-Shy . . . at last I've found true love.

Song 4 (*Princess*)

At the end of the song, Aladdin enters down R *furtively*

The Handmaidens give little shrieks of surprise and attempt to hide the Princess. She brushes them aside

Aladdin. (*She hurries to him*) How on earth did you manage to get into the Palace gardens?

Aladdin Simple. I climbed the wall.

So-Shy (*anxiously*) If he's *caught* here, Your Highness . . .

Aladdin (*to the Princess*) I just had to see you again.

Princess (*quickly*) Wait. (*To So-Shy and others*) Keep watch for my father and the Imperial Guards. Warn us the moment they appear.

The Handmaidens exit in an excited flurry, but So-Shy goes reluctantly

Aladdin Oh, Princess. I've got the most marvellous news to tell you. Before very long I'm going to be one of the richest men in all China. And when *that* happens, I'm going to come straight here and ask your father for his permission to marry you.

Princess If only it were true.

Aladdin It *is*. I swear it. A long-lost uncle of mine has just turned up and he's going to take me to a place where jewels are so thick on the ground even *weeds* can't grow.

Princess (*amazed*) I've never heard of such a place.

Aladdin Nor I. But if he says he's going to take me there, how can I refuse? Oh, Princess . . . I can't wait for the day when we'll be married.

Princess And I feel the same. But now you really *must* go. Father will be here in a moment and if he catches us talking again . . .

Aladdin Don't worry. At the first warning of his approach, I'll be off like a shot.

So-Shy hurries in

So-Shy (*as she enters*) Princess . . . Princess. Your royal father . . .

Aladdin turns to run out but escape route is blocked as . . .

The Guards and the Vizier enter

Aladdin turns again, but . . .

The Emperor and other Guards face him. Handmaidens etc. crowd on

Emperor (*seeing Aladdin*) So. You're at it again, are you? Well this time we won't chop off your head ... we'll chop off your *body*. (*To the Guards*) Seize him.

Before anyone can move, Abanazar enters down L

Abanazar (*loudly*) Stop.

Everyone looks at him, startled

Abracadabra ... Abracadeeze ... by the power of this ring I command you to freeze.

Everyone but Aladdin suddenly goes rigid

Aladdin Uncle Abanazar. You saved my life. But what are you doing here?

Abanazar Foolish boy. With the aid of my magic powers I watched you from afar. When I saw your danger, I hurried to save you. Now come.

Aladdin Magic powers?? (*He looks at everyone in awe*) But what about the Princess and everyone else? They look like Madame Tussaud's waxworks.

Abanazar (*sourly*) More like a meeting of the (*local town council*).

Aladdin How long will they stay like that?

Abanazar (*impatiently*) A few moments only. Now hurry. Return to your wretched home and bid farewell to your mother. We must leave for the cave at once.

Aladdin (*delighted*) Now? Oh, Uncle. You don't know how happy you've made me. By this time tomorrow I'll have enough money to marry the Princess.

Abanazar By this time tomorrow, you'll be dea——(*he remembers himself*)—decidedly richer. Now hurry or it will be too late.

Aladdin (*to the Princess*) I don't know if you can hear me or not ... but don't worry. I'll be back tomorrow. (*He kisses her lightly on the cheek*)

Aladdin exits quickly

Abanazar (*gazing after him with a sneer*) You little fool. You'll never return to Peking. Your bones will rot beneath the ground until the end of time ... whilst I ... Abanazar ... take my rightful place as Master of the Universe.

He gives a harsh laugh and exits

As he does, there is a quick fade to Black-out

SCENE 4

Behind the Laundry. A lane scene

Wishee enters

Wishee Hiya, kids. Here ... I've got to tell you this. I got that job in the laundry. Starting this afternoon. I'm going to be the chief button-crusher.

Hey . . . and what about that old woman who runs it? Aladdin's mother. What a face. Do you know, last night she was getting ready for bed . . . and a Peeping Tom reached inside the window and pulled the curtains shut. It's true. She's the only woman *I've* ever heard of who can walk into a room and make the *mice* jump on to the chairs. (*He chuckles*) Mind you, looks aren't everything, are they? Course they're not. In *her* case they aren't anything. (*He laughs*)

The Babes enter looking downcast

Here . . . what's the matter? Why are you looking so miserable?

Babe 1 We've just heard the news. You've got yourself a job and won't be here to join in our games any more.

Wishee Ohhhh. Well *I'm* sorry about that, too . . . but grown-ups have to go to work, you know.

Babe 2 Why?

Wishee Well . . . a grown-up goes to work to earn money. And if he gets to work early every day, and works hard, and leaves late . . . he might get a better position . . . and if he *does* . . . and he starts even earlier, works even harder and finishes even later . . . he can earn lots and lots of money. And when he's earned lots and lots of money . . . he'll be able to stop working, stay at home, and do nothing all day long for the rest of his life.

Babe 3 But *you* do that now, so why waste time working?

Wishee (*after a reaction*) Anyway . . . you don't have to worry. I'll always have time to join in your games. 'Cos you're my mates, aren't you? And mates always have time for things like that. So come on. Cheer up. It's a smashing day and there's lots to be happy about. Stick a smile on your faces and start singing. There's nothing like a song to chase the blues away.

Song 5 (*Wishee and the Babes*)

At the end of the song, all march off cheerfully

The Lights fade for the end of the scene

SCENE 5

Widow Twankey's Chinese Laundry

Full lighting. A very large washing machine is set CB (see Production Note) and a large box of "Instant Shrink Washing Powder" stands beside it. A large blackboard and easel is up L, and on this is written various names of customers and what they owe. An eraser and chalk are to hand. Two baskets of dirty washing are R

When the scene begins, the Laundry Workers are enjoying themselves in a dance routine utilizing various items of laundry

Song 6 (*Laundry workers*)

At the end of the song, Widow Twankey enters R, *briskly*

Twankey (*clapping her hands dismissively*) Go on. Scram. The lot of you. There's no time for enjoying yourselves. We've got work to do.

Everyone scurries out

Now then ... where's my new assistant, Wishee Washee? (*She calls*) Wishee?

Wishee enters with an "L" plate on his back

Wishee Hiya, kids. (*To Twankey*) Here I am, Mrs Twankey. All ready and willing. (*He stops dead in his tracks*) Blimey.
Twankey (*startled*) What's wrong?
Wishee It's you. You look different. Younger.
Twankey (*flattered*) Do I? (*She simpers*) Well ... it's very kind of you to say so ... but I have to be honest. I'm not the woman I was ten years ago.
Wishee How's that?
Twankey Well I'm a year older, to begin with. But never mind that. I think I'm going to like you. You're just my kind of man. You're available. Now ... before we start work, there's just one or two questions I want to ask you. To start with ... you don't have trouble with lumbago, do you?
Wishee Lumbago? No, Mrs Twankey.
Twankey Good. Because my late husband *died* from the results of lumbago.
Wishee Gerraway. You can't die from lumbago.
Twankey *He* did. We had to rub whisky on his back to ease the pain, and he broke his neck trying to lick it off. Anyway ... the next thing I want to know is what you're doing looking for work in *this* part of the city? Why did you leave your home behind?
Wishee Well ... it was too big to carry.
Twankey (*after a reaction*) And finally ... how good are you at maths? You see there's a lot of arithmetic involved in this job.
Wishee Oh, I'm very good at maths, Mrs Twankey. You test me and see.
Twankey All right, then. I will. Two shirts at one pound fifty pence each?
Wishee Three pounds.
Twankey Four pair of trousers at sixty pence?
Wishee Two pounds forty.
Twankey Thirteen starched collars at seven pence each?
Wishee Twenty-eight pence.
Twankey Six pairs of ladies'——(*she realizes*). Just a minute. Just a minute. What do you mean, twenty-eight pence? How can seven thirteens be twenty-eight?
Wishee (*puzzled*) But they are, Mrs Twankey. Always have been.
Twankey Oh, no they haven't.
Wishee Oh, yes they have ... and I'll prove it. (*He cleans the blackboard and picks up the chalk*) Thirteen multiplied by seven. (*He writes a large 13 on the board and an equally large 7 beneath the figure 3*) Now then ... three sevens are twenty-one. That's two down and one to carry. (*He writes the*

figure 2) Seven ones are seven ... and this one makes eight. (*He writes down the 8*) Seven thirteens make twenty-eight.

Twankey That's not right. You've got everything mixed up. Look ... *divide* twenty-eight by seven and you'll see where you went wrong ...

Wishee All right. (*He cleans the board*) Twenty-eight divided by seven. (*He writes it down so: 7/ 28*) Seven into two won't go ... so put the two to one side. (*He writes down the 2 at a distance*) Seven into eight goes one ... (*he writes it down*) ... and there's one left over. One and two make three ... (*He writes it next to the 1*) So seven into twenty-eight is thirteen.

Twankey No, no, no. It isn't, it isn't, it isn't. Write thirteen down seven times and *add* it up. That way you can't go wrong.

Wishee Add it up. (*He cleans the board and writes down seven 13s in a column*) Now all the boys and girls add it up with me. (*He counts*) Three ... six ... nine ... twelve ... fifteen ... eighteen ... twenty-one ... (*He counts the 1s now*) Twenty-two ... twenty-three ... twenty-four ... twenty-five ... twenty-six ... twenty-seven ... twenty-eight.

Twankey Oh, I give up. They're as daft as you are. Come on. Put that chalk down and let's sort out this washing. Oh ... and remember ... you've got to be careful with these things. They belong to some very important people.

Wishee Do they? (*He picks up a large pair of bloomers with a padlock and chain attached to them*) Oh, yes ... Mrs Mary Whitehouse. (*He tosses them aside and picks up another pair made out of an old flag*) And Maggie Thatcher's.

Twankey (*snatching them off him*) Give over. They're very precious, these are. There's been many a battle fought under this flag.

Wishee (*holding up a pair of stockings with no feet to them*) Here ... what use are these? There's no feet in 'em.

Twankey Well of course there isn't. They're special stockings that folks wear when they want to walk up muddy lanes. You just pull 'em up your legs and that way it's only your feet that get dirty.

Wishee And what's these? (*He picks up a pair of long johns*)

Twankey Well ... (*She glances around to make sure she is not overheard*) They're underpants belonging to one of the angels. They've got his name in the back.

Wishee (*looking*) Ooh, yes. St Michael. (*He puts them down*) Here, Mrs Twankey, there's certainly an awful lot of washing to do.

Twankey Never mind. Tip it all into the washing machine.

They put the laundry into the machine

And plenty of washing powder on top of it.

Wishee shakes a huge amount of powder into the machine

Wishee (*peering inside*) Hey ... I think there's too many clothes in it, Mrs Twankey. The water isn't covering them.

Twankey (*turning away*) Well press 'em down then. Press 'em down. (*She moves down to the other basket*)

Wishee reaches down and presses on the washing. He loses his balance and falls headfirst into the machine)

(*Not noticing*) Then after you've done that, you can come over here and help me with this lot. (*She beams*) Oh, it is nice having a man around the place again. (*To the audience*) I'll tell you this, girls ... when that man walked in here this morning, I took one look at him and ... (*She glances round and sees he is missing*) Wishee? (*She looks around*) Wishee??? (*Puzzled*) That's funny. (*She thinks*) Oh, yes ... he'll have gone to put the kettle on. I'll make a start with the ironing. (*She turns back to the second basket and stoops to pick it up*)

Aladdin enters cheerily behind her and slaps her on the bottom

(*Delightedly*) Oooh ... I'll have two extra pints, please. (*She turns and sees Aladdin*) Oh, Aladdin. Where've *you* been?

Aladdin I'll tell you later, Mum ... but listen. I've got the most exciting news to tell you. Uncle Abanazar's taking me to the cave of jewels tonight. I've just come to say cheerio.

Twankey But ... but you're not going right now, are you? Not this minute? I mean ... what about your supper? I've got your favourite meal ready for you. Senna pod casserole.

Aladdin Sorry, Mum.

Twankey Well shall I save it for you? Till you get back?

Aladdin No thanks, Mum. When I get back from that cave, there'll be no casserole for us ever again. It'll be champagne and caviar for the rest of our lives.

Twankey (*doubtfully*) I don't know. I'm not sure I entirely trust that uncle of yours. He's so sugary sweet you could get diabetes just *listening* to him.

Aladdin Oh, don't fuss, Mum. I can take care of myself. I'm a big boy now. (*He begins to exit*) Well ... cheerio.

Twankey Here ... you're not going like *that*, are you? (*She points at his trousers*)

Aladdin Why not? (*He feels the back of his trousers*) Oh, there's a hole in my trousers. How did that get there?

Twankey I don't know, but I shall have to look into it. Hang on a minute. I'll go and get my darning things.

She exits quickly and returns with a small darning box (containing a pre-threaded large needle) and a small stool

Come on. (*She puts the stool down and sits on it*) Over my knee.

Aladdin positions himself across her knees

Now you've got your clean underwear on, haven't you? Just in case you get knocked down.

Aladdin Oh, Mum ...

Twankey Never mind "Oh, Mum". (*She gets the needle out and begins to sew*) You can't be too careful, these days. And if anything *did* happen to you ... I don't know what I'd do. (*She sniffles*)

Aladdin *Nothing's* going to happen to me, Mum.
Twankey That's what your grandmother said just before she ate that slice
of Trusthouse Forte coffee. And look what happened to *her*. Oh, I know
I'm just being a silly old woman ... but without you, life wouldn't be
worth living. You're all I've got now, Aladdin. You're my everything.

Song 7 (*Twankey*)

*At the end of the song, she pats his bottom to indicate she has finished sewing,
and breaks the thread. Aladdin slides off her knees and hugs her gently*

Aladdin Thanks, Mum. And don't worry. I'll take care of myself.

*He moves away ... only to discover she has sewn her skirt firmly to his
trousers. Reaction from both. Twankey cuts the thread to separate them. A cry
from Wishee is heard*

Twankey (*startled*) What's that?
Aladdin It sounds like Wishee ... and it's coming from the washing
machine.

*They hurry to the washing machine, peer inside and lift out one of the Babes
dressed in Wishee's costume, clutching the box of washing powder*

The Babe runs off as—

Twankey faints into Aladdin's arms. Black-out

SCENE 6

A rocky pass in the mountains

*A lane scene depicting a boulder strewn pass in the mountains. The cave
entrance is concealed by a large boulder R. Subdued lighting*

Wishee enters in outrageous "pop singer" outfit. A spotlight picks him out

Wishee Hiya, kids. Ooh, aren't I glad to be back to normal again. Here ...
what do you think of the outfit? (*He parades it*) I bet you're wondering
what I'm doing all dressed up like this, aren't you? Well I'll tell you.
Seeing as how poor old Widow Twankey hasn't got any money, I thought
I'd try and help her. So I've decided to become a pop singer. Well ...
everybody knows that pop singers make a lot of money, don't they ...
especially the ones who can't sing at all. Anyway ... I've come up here
into the mountains to do a bit of practising, 'cos there's some marvellous
echoes ... and as a special favour ... you can all sit there and listen to me
rehearsing. Would you like that? Would you?

Audience reaction

All right, then. I'm going to start now ... and if *you* want to help me out, I
came in that way. (*He indicates*)

Song 8 (*Wishee; possible audience participation*)

At the end of the song, Wishee exits cheerily

As the spot blacks out, Abanazar enters opposite, fuming. A green spot picks him out

Abanazar Still no sign of that wretched cave, and the top of the mountain is almost in view. Are my plans to end in failure?

Aladdin enters

Aladdin (*wearily*) Oh, Uncle. My feet are killing me. How much further is it to this secret cave of yours?

Abanazar (*trying to laugh it off*) Not *much* further, my little nephew. In fact ... we should almost be on top of the place by now.

Aladdin You don't sound very sure.

Abanazar (*snarling*) Of course I'm not sure, you stupid little——(*He recovers*) Ahem ... I mean ... so many of these passes seem the same at night.

Aladdin You're telling me ... and we must have walked up every one of them. Surely there must be something particular to watch out for? An old tree stump ... or an odd-shaped boulder.

Abanazar   You see that mystic pattern formed
(*pointing upwards*)   By stars way out in space?
                            Carved on a boulder seek its twin ...
                            For 'neath it lies the place.

Aladdin (*after a glance*) What's that over there? (*He indicates the large boulder* R) Half covered with moss.

Abanazar (*eagerly*) Where? (*He hurries to it and rubs at the moss*) You're right. It *is*. We've found it. We've *found* it. (*He laughs in triumph*)

Aladdin I don't know what you're getting all excited about. We'll need a stick of dynamite to shift *that*.

Abanazar Have you forgotten my magic powers? (*Grandly*) Stand aside.

Aladdin moves back

Abracadabra, abracadee, open magic cave for *me*. (*He casts a spell*)

There is a great rumble and the boulder rolls to one side revealing a dark hole

At last. At last. (*To Aladdin*) Quickly, boy. Into the cave.

Aladdin (*peering into it*) It's awfully dark in there.

Abanazar (*sneering*) You're not *scared*, are you?

Aladdin Of course not. It's just that ... well ... I don't understand why you're giving *me* all the jewels and things, and all *you* want is a dusty old lamp.

Abanazar But I explained on the way here. I'm so rich I don't *need* any more money and the lamp is an old one I've decided to give to Oxfam. All you have to do is pass it up to me.

Aladdin Why don't you go down and get it for yourself?

Abanazar Because ... because I have a bad leg. (*He clutches it*) I can't climb up and down rocks so well these days.

Aladdin Oh, all right. I'll get it for you. (*He enters the cave*)
Abanazar (*delighted*) He's in. He's in.
Aladdin (*re-emerging*) I'm out. I'm out.
Abanazar (*furiously*) Ten thousand curses. What's the matter now?
Aladdin Oh, Uncle. I *am* a *bit* scared. What if there's a dreadful monster down there?
Abanazar Nonsense. It's just an ordinary cave. Now get in there and bring me that lamp.
Aladdin All right. All right. There's no need to shout. (*He begins to exit but comes back*) But what if there *is* something down there to frighten me?
Abanazar I tell you there *isn't*. (*Exasperated*) Look . . . (*He tears the ring off his finger*) Take this magic ring of mine. (*He hands it over*) So long as you wear this, nothing can harm you. Now *go*.
Aladdin (*putting on the ring*) Well . . .
Abanazar Think of your Princess, Aladdin. *Think* of her.
Aladdin You're right. I'll do it for her.

He exits into the cave

Abanazar (*peering inside anxiously*) Watch your step, boy. Look out for loose rocks.
Aladdin (*off*) I will.

Abanazar swirls away from the entrance with an evil laugh, and moves c. The Lights fade all around him until only his face and shoulders are visible

Abanazar Poor trusting fool. Little does he know that once that Lamp is in my hands, I'll have no further use for him. (*He laughs harshly*) O mighty Gods . . . I thank thee for granting me possession of the ancient Lamp of power. At last my quest is ended, and before the sun's first rays can light the sky, the whole world will tremble at the sound of my name. Abanazar . . . Abanazar . . . ABANAZAR.

As he speaks the last three words, the light on him begins to fade. The last word is spoken in complete darkness

SCENE 7

Inside the Magic Cave

A vast cavern interior, lit with blues, green and reds. Its rocky walls are bare, no glimpse of jewels are to be seen. The Lamp is on a small rock R

As the scene begins, Aladdin is stepping off a large rock on to the cavern floor. The opening to the cave is visible high above his head

Aladdin (*gazing around nervously*) What a spooky place . . . and so dark. (*He moves downstage*) I don't see any sign of the jewels Uncle Abanazar mentioned. This *is* the right place, I suppose? I'd better give him a call. (*Calling*) Uncle? Uncle Abanazar?

Abanazar appears at the entrance

Abanazar Yes, yes? Do you have it? Is it there?

Aladdin Honestly ... talk about a one-track mind. I can't see any jewels down here.

Abanazar (*snapping*) Of course there are jewels. Look behind the rocks ... but first ... pass me the Lamp. (*He holds out his hand for it*)

Aladdin Hang on a minute. I haven't even found it, yet. (*He sees it*) Oh ... here it is. (*He picks it up*) What a tatty old thing.

Abanazar (*eagerly*) Quick, quick. Give it to me.

Aladdin Don't be so *eager*. Wait till I've found the jewels. (*He looks round*)

Abanazar A curse on the jewels. Give me the *Lamp*.

Aladdin (*annoyed*) I won't give you anything if you're going to shout at me.

Abanazar (*softening his voice*) Very well ... (*his voice rising*) ... but will you stop wasting time and—(*he screams*)—give me that Lamp.

Aladdin (*piqued*) No.

Abanazar (*furiously*) Give it to me.

Aladdin Not till I find the jewels. (*To the audience*) You know ... there's something very funny going on here. I don't believe there's any jewels in this cave at all.

Abanazar (*with great menace*) Aladdin ... I'm warning you.

Aladdin You can warn as much as you like. I'm not coming out of this cave till I've filled my pockets with precious stones. And unless *that* happens you can whistle for your dirty old lamp. (*He puts it back on the rock*)

Abanazar (*thunderously*) Very well then. So be it. Stay inside and *die* there.

Aladdin (*startled*) What?

Abanazar (*raising his arm*) Hocus Pokus, magic door ... hold him fast for evermore.

There is a flash and a loud rumble as the entrance to the cave is sealed

Aladdin (*horrified*) Uncle. Uncle. I was only joking. Let me out. I'll give you the Lamp if you want it. (*He snatches it up and hurries to below the cave entrance*) Uncle ... come back. Please.

There is absolute silence. In a daze, Aladdin moves down C

He's gone. Locked me in. Left me here to die. What am I going to do? I'll never escape from this dreadful place. Never. (*He wipes his eye with his ring hand*) Ouch ... (*Realizing*) The ring. Uncle Abanazar's magic ring. I'd forgotten all about that. Oh ... if only I knew how to make it work. (*Nervously he rubs his hand across the ring*)

There is a flash and the Slave of the Ring appears

(*Startled*) Ooooh. (*He steps back in fright*)

Slave What is thy wish, O master? (*He bows deeply*)

Aladdin M ... master? Er ... who are *you*?

Slave I am the Slave of the Magic Ring, O master, and here to do thy bidding.

Aladdin You mean ... you'll do anything I ask? Then please ... please take me out of this horrible place.

Slave Alas ... I do not have the power to break this rocky shape ...

But in your hand, O master, is the key to your escape.
That Lamp is an object of infinite power ...
For centuries sleeping, awaiting this hour.
When used by a person who's honest and true
And free from all evil ... great good it can do.
But terrible harm will most surely be done
Should it come to the hands of a treacherous one.
So keep the Lamp safe, and you will possess
Great wisdom and wealth ... and your pretty Princess.

The Slave exits

Aladdin (*looking at the Lamp*) A magic lamp. No wonder Uncle Abanazar was so anxious to get his hands on it. But how does it work? Wait ... that looks like writing under the dust. Perhaps if I gave it a quick polish I could read what it says. (*He rubs the lamp briskly*)

There is a great flash and a crack of thunder. The Genie of the Lamp appears. A massive, muscular figure in the minimum of gold clothing to show off his figure

Genie What is they wish, O master? (*He salaams deeply*)

Aladdin (*awed at the sight of him*) Who are *you*?

Genie Master ... I am thy humble slave. The Genie of the Magic Lamp. For centuries I have awaited your coming, and now you are here for me to serve. All your wishes shall be fulfilled, for no power on earth is greater than mine. Command and I will obey.

Aladdin You will? In that case ... can you please get me out of this horrible cave?

Genie (*with a great laugh*) Nothing is simpler, O master. Come. (*He extends his hand*)

Aladdin (*hesitantly*) Er ... before we go, Mr Genie ... I don't suppose there *are* any jewels in this place?

Genie If jewels you want, O master, jewels you shall have. The riches of the world are yours for the asking. Cloths of gold and silver ... shimmering silks ... the rarest wines and spices ... fruits from the gardens of Allah himself. Come ... and whilst I show you the vast treasures of earth, the spirits of the cave shall conjure up sights that mortal man has never dreamed of.

Aladdin follows the Genie off. As they exit, a Ballet of the Jewels begins with dancers dressed as the various precious stones known to man. At a given point, the Spirits exit and Twankey and Wishee appear as principal ballerina and partner. They perform a balloon ballet, then exit. The Jewels now re-appear to present Aladdin as he re-enters with the Genie. Aladdin is now dressed in very spectacular clothing

Aladdin (*dazed*) Oh, Mr Genie ... I never knew such wealth existed in the world. Is it truely all mine?

Genie For as long as you hold the Magic Lamp, O master.

Aladdin (*firmly*) Then take me back home. To wealth and happiness.

To Mother . . . and Wishee . . . and my pretty Princess.
From this moment on, life is roses and wine . . .
I hold the Magic Lamp and the world is mine.

The Genie makes a sign. The cave entrance opens and the sun streams in. The Jewels form a picture as Aladdin begins the climb out. Halfway up the rocks, he turns and holds the Lamp aloft, and——

the CURTAIN *falls*

ACT II

SCENE 1

The Pleasure Gardens of Chou-En-Gum

A large pleasure garden in Chinese style, with pagoda and lakes visible. Princess Badroulbador and her Handmaidens, plus the Citizens of Peking are enjoying themselves with singing and dancing. As the Princess leads the song, others dance holding streamers and lanterns

Song 9 (*Princess and Choristers*)

After the song, Choristers fall back leaving Princess and So-Shy C

Princess (*breathlessly*) Oh, So-Shy . . . I can't remember when I've enjoyed myself so much. (*She laughs happily*) Thank goodness my father can't see me. He'd have a fit.

So-Shy Especially as you're making no attempt to hide your face from the crowd.

Princess I know. Isn't it terrible of me? (*She laughs*) Oh, I'm so tired of living in that stuffy old Palace with hardly anyone to talk to. It's much more interesting to be here in the Pleasure Gardens. Besides . . . if I'm lucky, I may just catch a glimpse of Aladdin.

So-Shy (*wide-eyed*) I don't know about Aladdin, Your Highness . . . but if you're not careful, you'll be getting a glimpse of your father. Look, he's heading this way. (*She indicates*)

Princess (*looking off; startled*) Quickly. Down the path to the boating lake.

With much giggling and excitement, all hurry off as the Emperor totters on up L

Emperor (*peering after them*) Badroulbador? Badroulbador?? (*He shakes his head*) No, no. It couldn't possibly be . . . and yet . . . and yet . . .

Twankey enters behind him

That exquisite figure . . .

Twankey reacts in pleasant surprise

Skin as pale as porcelain . . .

She reacts again and touches her cheek

Eyes like the summer skies . . .

She flutters her lashes

And hair like the purest silk.

Twankey feels her hair, grimaces, then shrugs

It *must* be her.

Twankey (*joyfully*) It *is*.

Emperor (*still gazing off*) I knew it. The sunshine of my life ... here in the Pleasure Gardens.

Twankey Oh, you saucy old devil. (*She slaps his back playfully and sends him reeling*)

Emperor (*outraged*) How dare you, madam? How *very* dare you? (*Recognizing her*) Widow Twankey.

Twankey (*beaming*) Oh, Your Mint Imperial ... there's no need for formalitude between us. Call me Titania and give me a kiss. (*She puckers her lips*)

Emperor (*indignantly moving back*) I certainly won't.

Twankey (*surprised*) Why not? (*Realizing*) Oh ... of course. (*She puts her finger to her lips*) It's "hush, hush" isn't it? You don't want the *Daily Mirror* to find out about us until we've made the official announcement.

Emperor What *are* you talking about, woman?

Twankey Our engagement.

Emperor Engagement? What engagement?

Twankey Well ... don't you want to marry me and make me your Empressario?

Emperor Certainly not.

Twankey But ... didn't you just say I was the sunshine of your life?

Emperor Of course I didn't. I was referring to my daughter.

Twankey (*hopefully*) And don't *I* remind you of your daughter?

Emperor You, madam ... remind me of the China sea.

Twankey (*brightening*) Because I'm wild, exotic and restless?

Emperor No. Because you make me *sick*.

Twankey (*to the audience*) Oh, they can say what they like about him, but he certainly knows how to pay a lady compliments. (*To Emperor*) Here ... how would you like to take me to (*she names a local Chinese restaurant*) for a plateful of Kung Fu Yung?

Emperor Kung Fu Yung? Whatever's that?

Twankey Well ... it's like Egg Fu Yung ... but you have to wrestle the waiter for it.

Emperor Bah. Enough of this nonsense. Where's that son of yours, Aladdin?

Twankey Don't ask me. He went off with his Uncle Avabanana last night and I haven't set eyes on him since.

Emperor (*annoyed*) Botheration.

Twankey (*remembering*) Here ... you're not still wanting to chop his head off, are you?

Emperor Never you mind. But I want to know the minute he arrives back. Understand?

He snaps his fan open and totters off

Twankey Oh, blimey. I was hoping he'd have forgotten about it by now. Well ... He's not all that bright, you know. He went into (*local department store*) last week, and at the bottom of the moving staircase he saw a big notice ... "Dogs must be carried". It took him two hours to find one he could lift. And *absent-minded*? He left a note on the Palace door once saying "Back in an hour" ... and when he returned, he read it, thought it over, and sat down and waited. Still ... we shouldn't mock the affiliated, should we? I mean ... it could happen to any of us. Take me, for instance ... I'm so worried about my Aladdin, I can hardly think straight. I didn't sleep a wink last night. At half-past four this morning, I was sitting up in bed ... wide-awake ... oiling the rollers on the vacuum cleaner ... and there was this terrible hammering on the bedroom door. Ohhhhh. I was *terrified*. It's a wonder it didn't have half the neighbourhood awake. What a noise. (*Confidentially*) It was my new assistant, Wishee Washee. (*She nods*) I had to get up in the finish and let him out. (*Innocently*) Well ... it's an outside toilet, you see, and I always lock the back door for safety. Still ... I was so shattered this morning, I didn't even have the energy to scrub the woollens ... so I decided to come here for an hour or two and relax.

Wishee enters with a bunch of flowers and a shopping bag

Wishee Hiya, kids. Hello, Mrs Twankey. (*Admiringly*) Here ... I like your dress.
Twankey (*pleased*) Do you? (*She simpers*) Here ... well I'll tell you a little secret. This dress is over a hundred and fifty years old. (*She smirks*)
Wishee (*awed*) Cor ... and did you make it yourself?
Twankey (*annoyed*) No, I didn't make it myself. Anyway ... what are *you* doing here? You're supposed to be back in the laundry bleaching the coloured stuff.
Wishee Yes, I know. But you've been so nice to me ... giving me a job and letting me come to live with you ... I thought I'd just nip out and buy you some flowers. (*He shows her the bunch of flowers*)
Twankey (*overcome*) Oh ... aren't they beautiful? (*Simpering and pursing her lips in a large O*) This is for the flowers.
Wishee Don't be silly. You must have a vase at home, somewhere.
Twankey (*wincing*) Oooooh.
Wishee Here ... and I've got something else for you, too. (*He hands her the bag*)
Twankey (*peering eagerly inside it*) Oh ... what is it?
Wishee Something *really* special. A papier-mâché kettle.
Twankey Papier mâché *kettle*?? What use is *that*?
Wishee It's the very latest thing, Mrs Twankey. It's a *safety* kettle. You see ... it can't boil over. If ever it gets too hot, it just burns away and the water puts the flames out.
Twankey (*after a wince*) Well ... I suppose this means you want to marry me, does it?
Wishee (*startled*) Eh? How do you work that out?
Twankey (*airily*) Oh, I know what it means all right when men start buying

presents. You're all alike ... thank goodness. One look at a beautiful woman and you can't wait to propose to her. (*Smugly*) Oooh, if I had a penny for every man who's wanted to marry *me* ...

Wishee (*to the audience*) She'd buy a stick of liquorice.

Twankey Even that Grand Vizier feller's chasing after me, you know. Gave me a beautiful engagement ring. I couldn't *wait* to get down to the Women's Institute so everybody could admire it.

Wishee And did they?

Twankey Not really ... but six of them *recognized* it. Still ... I had to turn him down. I'm a very respectable woman, I am, and I didn't want to marry a man who knew such a lot of naughty rude songs.

Wishee (*puzzled*) Naughty rude songs, Mrs Twankey? *I've* never heard the Grand Vizier singing naughty rude songs.

Twankey No ... but you can certainly hear him *whistling* them. Anyway ... never mind about him. Let's go and watch the knife-thrower in the circus tent while I decide whether to accept your proposal or not.

Wishee Oh ... I'd rather we didn't, Mrs Twankey. I saw that knife-thrower yesterday and he isn't very good at all. He must have thrown fifty knives at that girl assistant of his and never hit her once.

Twankey Well ... all right, then. I was only trying to keep you in suspenders a bit longer. If you can keep me in a manner to which I'm willing to become accustomed ... I'll marry you.

Wishee But ... but ... I *can't* marry you, Mrs Twankey. I haven't a penny in the world. I couldn't keep a mouse.

Twankey Of course you could. You can keep as many as you like. I love mice. (*Gleefully*) Oh, Wishee ... I just knew this was going to be a wonderful day. The minute I looked up into beautiful blue sky this morning, I said to myself ... (*She looks upwards*) Owwwwwww. (*She clutches at her eye*)

Wishee (*startled*) What's wrong?

Twankey (*wiping her eye*) I've just had a message from the Bluebird of Happiness.

Wishee (*trying to hide his grin*) Shall I get you some toilet paper?

Twankey What use would *that* be? The thing'll be miles away by now. (*She brightens*) Still ... you know what they say when something like that happens to you, don't you? They say you're a very lucky person.

Wishee Yes. You're very lucky that *cows* don't fly.

Twankey (*excitedly*) Oh, I can't wait to see Aladdin's face when I tell him he's going to have a new daddy. I'd better get back to the laundry and tidy a few things up. I don't want the place to look a mess when the wedding guests start arriving.

She giggles, blows kisses and exits

Wishee (*worried*) Oh, blimey. That's torn it. I can't afford to get married. Not yet, anyway. What am I going to do? (*He moves down* R)

Abanazar enters down L *stealthily*

Abanazar (*to himself*) May the curse of the ten thousand fleas from a diseased, one-eyed camel-driver's armpit fall upon the house of Twankey. The Magic Lamp is lost to me once more. But I'm not beaten yet. Somewhere in this accursed city there must be another simple-minded Chinaman ... another idiot I can persuade to do my bidding. But where? (*He notices Wishee*) Aha ... he looks a likely candidate. I'll approach him. (*He moves to Wishee and taps him on the shoulder*) Young man.

Wishee (*turning*) Eh?

Abanazar (*putting his arm round Wishee's shoulder*) Tell me ... how would you like to make a lot of money in a short time?

Wishee (*pulling away*) Gerroff. (*He glares at him*)

Abanazar (*quickly*) No, no. I mean ... are you interested in becoming very rich?

Wishee Oh. Ooh, yes. Not half. If I get rich, I'd be able to marry my fiasco.

Abanazar Fiasco? (*He smiles*) Surely you mean ... fiancée?

Wishee I know what I mean.

Abanazar Ho, ho. Quite a little joker, aren't you? But we have no time for joking if you wish to make your fortune. We must head for a secret cave in yonder mountains. (*He indicates off*)

Wishee (*wide-eyed*) Secret cave?

Abanazar Filled with jewels and riches beyond belief.

Wishee (*impressed*) Cor. Here ... wait a minute, though. I haven't got to steal anything, have I?

Abanazar No, no. Of course you haven't to steal anything. I promise you won't be involved in anything illegal.

Wishee (*blankly*) In what?

Abanazar Illegal. You ... er ... you *do* know what illegal means, don't you?

Wishee Course I do. I'm not daft, you know. Illegal is a sick bird.

Abanazar (*wincing*) Come ... we'll begin our journey before you have time to think of any more appalling puns like that.

Wishee Oh, it's not me that thinks them up. It's the scriptwriter. But hang on a minute. Before I go with you, I'll have to pop back to the laundry and tell Mrs Twankey I'm taking the afternoon off.

Abanazar (*aghast*) Twankey? Did you say *Twankey*? (*Furiously*) Of all the people in Peking, I have to choose one who knows the boy's mother. Ten thousand curses.

Wishee (*blankly*) Is something wrong?

Abanazar No, no. Not a thing. It's just that I ... er ... I seem to have made a slight *mistake*. The man *I* am looking for would never be found working in a laundry. He'd be a man of great *animal* attraction.

Wishee *I've* got animal attraction. Everywhere I go, dogs follow me around.

Abanazar I'm sorry. Some other time, perhaps ...

He turns to exit but comes face to face with Aladdin who is entering in rich clothing and carrying the Lamp

Aghhhhhh. (*He steps back in shock*)

Aladdin You. (*Quickly he rubs the Lamp*)

There is a flash and the Genie appears

Genie You summoned me, O master?
Aladdin Yes. (*He indicates Abanazar*) Take this verminous-looking object
and toss him into the nearest cess pool.
Abanazar (*horrified*) Noooooooooo.
Genie It shall be done, O master.

The Genie makes a signal. There is a Black-out

Genie and Abanazar vanish

The Lights come up again

Aladdin (*laughing*) That'll teach the old villain a lesson.
Wishee (*amazed*) Aladdin. Who was that feller in the gold Y-fronts . . . and
what are *you* doing dressed up like that? You're not going to be in an
amateur pantomime, are you?
Aladdin (*smiling*) I'll tell you all about it later, Wishee. Just for now, all I
want to say is you're looking at the richest man in the entire world.
Wishee (*worried*) Blimey. He's got sunstroke.
Aladdin Go find the Grand Vizier and bid him prepare a suitable reception
for a mighty Prince who even now approaches the city . . . laden with
fabulous gifts for the Emperor. If all goes well, before nightfall, the
earth's greatest treasures will be laid at his feet and the beautiful.Princess
Badroulbador will be claimed in marriage.
Wishee Here . . . I hope you know what you're doing. If this is another of
your little jokes . . .
Aladdin It's no joke, Wishee. From now on, everyone in China is going to
know my name. I'll put an end to misery and injustice . . . and everything
else that makes people unhappy. For this is my moment . . . the moment
I've waited for my entire life . . . and I'm going to do great things.

Song 10 (*Aladdin*)

As Aladdin sings, Wishee exits uncertainly

The Lights fade around Aladdin until only his head and shoulders are visible

At the end of the song there is a Black-out and Aladdin exits

SCENE 2

A quiet street

As Act 1, Scene 1

The Princess and her Handmaidens enter in a flurry

Princess (*glancing over her shoulder*) Do you think he saw us, So-Shy?
So-Shy (*breathlessly*) I don't think so, Your Highness, but all the same we'd
better be getting back to the Palace before you're missed. If anyone found
out you'd been to the Pleasure Gardens without an escort, I'm afraid we'd
all be punished.

All Handmaidens agree with nods

Princess (*giving a deep sigh*) Yes, I suppose you're right. But I *so* wanted to see Aladdin again.

So-Shy (*anxiously*) Your Highness. Don't even *whisper* his name in public. Someone may overhear.

Princess (*laughing*) Oh, So-Shy ... there's no need to look so worried. We're perfectly alone *here*.

The Vizier and some Guards enter

Vizier (*aghast*) Princess.

All react in confusion. The Guards throw up their arms to hide their eyes. Handmaidens and Princess are dismayed

(*Sternly*) Replace your veil at once and return to the Palace.

Princess Grand Vizier ...

Vizier (*insisting*) At once, I say.

The Princess veils her face and the Vizier gives a signal to the Guards. Quickly they move forward to escort the ladies

(*Concerned*) Oh, botheration. Whatever is the Emperor going to say about *this*?

So-Shy (*moving to him*) He won't say anything if you don't tell him. Oh, please, Mr Vizier ... it was only a bit of harmless fun.

Vizier (*grandly*) Fun? In *this* part of the world, Miss So-Shy, Princesses do not have *fun*. (*Weakening*) However ... in view of the circumstances ... perhaps "Least said, soonest mended". Return to the Palace and we'll forget the incident ever occurred.

Princess (*relieved*) Oh, thank you, Grand Vizier. I always knew you couldn't be as grumpy and unfeeling as everyone says ... (*Realizing*) Oh ...

Vizier (*sighing*) Don't worry, Your Highness. I know I'm not exactly a popular figure around the Palace, but *somone* has to do the unpleasant jobs, haven't they? How exceedingly fortunate then that I enjoy my work so much.

Song 11 (*Vizier and Guards*)

At the end of the song, the Vizier gives a signal and the entire party move off to the Palace as the Lights quickly fade

SCENE 3

Back in the Laundry

As Act 1, Scene 5. Full lighting. Twankey is sitting on her little footstool up by the washing machine as Aladdin concludes the story of his adventure

Twankey (*eyes popping*) Well ... I've never heard such adventures in all my born days. Ooh . . . if I ever get my hands on that phoney uncle of yours, I'll tie a knot in his tongue and swing on it. (*She rises*)

Aladdin (*laughing*) Don't worry. I think we've seen the last of *him*. But look . . . I've brought you a little present back, too. (*He gets out a small leather sack*)

Twankey (*unsure*) It's not a stick of rock, is it? You know I can't get——

Aladdin (*interrupting*) No, no. Look. (*He pours jewels from the sack into her hands*) They were a gift from the Genie, and there's lots more where these came from.

Twankey (*dazed*) I can't believe it. I haven't seen so much lolly since I watched (*she names local council*) getting their expenses paid.

Aladdin Now there's no reason why I can't go to the Emperor and ask for his daughter's hand in marriage. After all . . . with the aid of my Magic Lamp, I'm even richer than *he* is.

Twankey (*looking at the Lamp*) It doesn't look very magic to me, dear. In fact it looks as though it could do with a bit of a polish. Here . . . hang on. I'll go get a duster and my tin of Brasso.

Aladdin (*amused*) There's no need for that, Mum. Look. I'll show you how it works. Here . . . (*He takes it from his belt and hands it to her*) Just give it a little rub with your hand.

Twankey (*cautiously*) You mean . . . like this? (*She rubs it gently*)

There is a flash and the Genie appears

Aghhhhhhhh. (*She lifts her dress to hide her face and shows her bloomers*)

Aladdin Don't be scared, Mother. He won't hurt you.

Twankey Cover him up, quickly. If Mary Whitehouse sees him, she'll have me laundry shut down.

Genie What is thy wish, O mistress?

Twankey (*peeping over her dress hem*) Eh?

Genie I come to do your will.

Twankey My Will? (*In a panic*) Oh, Aladdin. Call him off. I'm not making a Will out yet. I'm not ready to go.

Aladdin (*amused*) He means . . . what would you like best in all the world, Mum?

Twankey Oh . . . (*She lowers here dress*) Well . . . I . . . er . . . I wouldn't mind a new frock for when summer comes. There was a lovely one in the Oxfam shop this morning. It was sort of . . . fuschia pink with orange lace round the bottom . . . green spotted sleeves with purple stripes . . . a plunging neckline . . . and an epileptic on each shoulder. Do you think I could have that one?

Aladdin Oh, Mum. From now on you can have anything you want. Wonderful clothes in the finest silks and satins. As the Princess's mother-in-law, nothing will be too good for you.

Twankey That's what your father used to say, but he emphasized it differently.

Aladdin Now before I go to the Palace, there's something I have to do.

Twankey Yes. I think I should have done one, as well. I had three cups of tea during the interval.

Aladdin (*to the Genie*) Genie . . . can you build me a beautiful palace? Fit for the greatest emperor on earth?
Genie Nothing is simpler, O master.
Twankey I'm sure it is . . . but answer the question.
Genie (*bowing*) The task is finished, O master. (*He indicates off*)

Aladdin and Twankey gaze off in astonishment

Twankey Ooooooh. What a beautiful Bingo Hall it'd make. Here . . . is that going to be our new lodgings?
Aladdin It certainly is. Oh, Mother, isn't it magnificent? Now *I'm* off to see the Emperor. You join me as soon as you've decided what to wear. Look after her, Genie. See you later.

Aladdin exits cheerily

Twankey waves him off, then turns to sneak a look at the Genie who still stands, arms folded, waiting

Twankey (*eyes crossing*) Ooooooooooh. (*She moves downstage to talk to the audience*) Oh, girls . . . What a shock *he* gave me when he arrived. I didn't know where to look . . . first. (*She sneaks another look*) He looks just like a cream cake when you're on a strict diet. Phew . . . (*She fans herself*) Oh, I'm all hot and bothered. (*Confidentially*) Does he remind you of your husband, girls? Reminds me of *mine*. Not that old Twankey ever looked like *that*. Oh, no. He was so thin, every time he took his clothes off, it was like watching the unveiling of a walking stick. Mind you . . . he was very proud of his physique . . . Even won a fancy-dress costume competition with it. Yes. He swallowed a tomato juice and went as a thermometer. (*She sneaks another look*) Seems like a nice boy. (*To the Genie*) Excuse me . . . but aren't you cold standing around like that?

The Genie shakes his head

(*To the audience*) Just the same as Twankey. He never felt the cold either. Oh . . . I tell a lie. He did *once*. We went to a nudist colony in (*she names local district*) Yes. It was mid-winter and he got so cold, he had to grow a long beard before he could go down to Tesco's to do the shopping. Mind you . . . we didn't stay there for long. We got thrown out for putting dressing on the salad. (*To the Genie*) Are you *sure* you wouldn't like something warm to wrap round you? Me, for instance?

The Genie shakes his head again

Oh, all right. I'll let you get back to the dressing-room. How long will it take you to conjure up a real eye-popping frock, and make me young and beautiful again?
Genie The dress will take but the twinkling of an eye . . . but as for making you young and beautiful . . . alas . . . my powers are not that great.
Twankey (*to the audience*) You see? Everybody wants to be a comic in this show. (*To Genie*) Get out of it, you turbaned twerp. Go bring me the frock while I get rid of *these* old things.

Genie Your wish is my command.

The Genie exits

Twankey performs a comic strip-tease which is followed by a Black-out for the end of the scene

SCENE 4

The boudoir of the Princess. Evening

The Princess enters dabbing at her eyes

Princess (*bitterly*) What a fool I was to believe that he loved me. All day long I've waited for him to return as he promised, but now the night falls and there's still no sign of him. (*Sobbing*) Oh, Aladdin . . . was our love only a game to you?

So-Shy enters quietly

So-Shy Your Highness . . .

The Princess wipes her tears away

A great caravan of horses and camels is approaching the Palace . . . laden with gold and jewels.

Princess Fat Prince Pekoe again, I suppose. Still hoping I'll change my mind and marry him.

So-Shy Your royal father commands that you join him in the throne-room to greet the visitor.

Princess (*sadly*) Very well, So-Shy. Tell him I shall come at once.

So-Shy exits silently

If it is the will of Buddah that I marry Prince Pekoe, then so be it. But my heart will never forget the foolish dream of love it once held for a poor peasant boy.

Song 12 (*Princess*)

At the end of the song, she exits slowly and sadly as the Lights fade

SCENE 5

The Emperor's Throne-room

A magnificent hall. The ornate throne is c, and a very large comfortable cushion is on the floor beside it. The Emperor is sitting on the throne surrounded by Guards and Handmaidens. Other Handmaidens (or entertainers) are performing a short dance. At the end of the entertainment, the Emperor pulls himself to his feet looking agitated

Emperor Where *is* the girl? Our visitor will be here before *she* is. (*Glancing off as though looking through a window*) Ohhhhh. Just look at that sight. Jewels glinting in the lantern lights ... golden dishes illuminated by the moon. Whoever this mysterious Prince is, he must be almost as wealthy as a Trade Union leader.

The Princess enters looking downcast

Ah, there you are, Badroulbador. Quickly. Settle yourself beside me. You're only just in time.

He re-seats himself. The Princess seats herself on the large cushion, eyes downcast

Processional music begins and the Babes enter carrying gold and silver dishes piled high with jewels. They are followed by male and female slaves carrying larger dishes, etc. At the end of the procession come Twankey and Wishee ... both in outrageous costumes

Wishee Hiya, kids. (*Looking round*) So this is what the inside of (*he names a local bookmakers*) looks like?
Emperor (*startled*) Widow Twankey. (*Rising*) Don't tell me *you're* a member of this royal entourage?
Twankey I certainly am ... and so's Wishee. (*She beams*) Sorry we're late, Your Cholesterol Highness ... but I had to pop into Boots for some aspirin.
Emperor Oh? Did you have a headache?
Twankey Yes. I was putting some toilet water behind my ears, and the seat fell down and clobbered me.
Emperor (*looking at the jewels*) But ... but ... what have all these jewels to do with you two? I've never seen anything like them in my life.
Twankey (*airily*) Oh, these aren't anything. Just a few odds and ends we had lying around the place.
Emperor You mean ... they belong to *you*? (*He snorts*) Bah. Utter nonsense.
Wishee (*indignantly*) Here, you. Less of the nasturtiums. We may only be dressed in *these* old rags ... (*he indicates their glittering costumes*) but it doesn't mean to say we're bankruptured. I bet we're the only house in China that has monogrammed tea-bags.
Emperor (*weakly*) Ohhhh. I'm coming all over unnecessary. Send for the Court Physician.

The Vizier enters down R

Vizier (*announcing*) His Royal Highness, Prince Aladdin.

Aladdin enters in splendour, the Lamp at his belt

Princess (*amazed*) Aladdin. (*She rises and hurries to him eagerly*)
Aladdin Princess. (*He embraces her*)

The Court reacts in astonishment

Emperor (*indignantly*) How dare you, sir? Unhand my daughter at once.

Princess But Father . . . don't you recognize him?

Emperor Of course I do. But I don't want a common peasant cuddling you in front of the whole Court.

Aladdin (*proudly*) *Once* a common peasant, Your Majesty . . . but now the richest man in the entire world, and here to claim your daughter's hand in marriage.

All look delighted with the exception of the Emperor

Emperor (*firmly*) No, no, no. Out of the question. I couldn't possibly allow . . . (*Realizing*) Did you say "richest man in the *world*"?

Twankey He certainly did.

Emperor Oh . . . well . . . in *that* case . . . (*He titters*) Of course you can marry her. Vizier . . . Champagne for everyone.

All look delighted

Now tell me . . . (*He titters*) Where will you pair of love-birds be going for your honeymoon?

Aladdin Well . . . we really hadn't thought about it yet, Your Majesty.

Wishee Oh . . . well you want to be very careful when you do. My sister went to Devon for *her* honeymoon. A place called Two Bridges. Later on, she had twins.

Vizier *My* sister went sailing on the river Forth in Scotland for *her* honeymoon . . . and she had quads.

Twankey (*thoughtfully*) In that case, they'd better stay well away from the Thousand Islands.

Aladdin (*laughing*) All right, Mum . . .
But now throughout the city let laughter hold sway
Whilst we all prepare for our great Wedding Day.

All cheer in delight. Aladdin and the Princess step forward as the Lights begin to fade. The lane curtain closes behind them. Spotlights come up on both as they separate. Aladdin to L, and the Princess to R. The other lighting fades to Black-out

Song 13 (*Aladdin and Princess*)

As the song fades away, the spots pinpoint to Black-out

Aladdin and the Princess exit

SCENE 6

The Gates of Aladdin's Palace

A lane cloth depicting a huge pair of ornamental gates through which can be seen a magnificent landscaped garden. It is daylight

Abanazar enters. The Lights dim

Abanazar So ... Aladdin and the Princess are married, are they? A thousand curses on them both. Here will they live in luxury whilst I roam the streets of the city in despair. (*Angrily*) By the toenails of the Prophet, I won't allow it. The Lamp is mine by rights and I intend to have it. (*To the audience*) *You'll* help me, won't you?

Audience reaction

No??? Very well, then. I'll do it myself. But how? How? (*He muses*) Wait ... I have it. (*He laughs harshly*) I shall return shortly. (*He gives another laugh*)

Abanazar exits rapidly

Twankey and Wishee enter. The Lights go back to normal

Twankey Ohhh, what a smashing party that was. Did you ever *see* such food? That Genie certainly knows how to cook.

Wishee I didn't think much of that roast centipede, though.

Twankey No ... but at least everybody got a leg. Mind you ... (*she glances around to make sure she is not being overheard*) there was a dead fly in my birds' nest soup.

Wishee Well what did you expect? A dead budgie?

Twankey Oh, but didn't they make a lovely pair, my Aladdin and the Princess? It took me right back to my own wedding day all those years ago. (*She dabs at her eyes*) I'll never forget standing there in front of the vicar and saying "I do" ... (*she winces*) and three fellers at the back shouting "Hear, hear". Oh, but he was a lovely man was old Twankey. Always paying me compliments.

Wishee Oh?

Twankey Every day he'd look at me and say "You're a nice one, aren't you?".

Wishee Do you still miss him, Mrs Twankey?

Twankey Oh, yes. In fact ... just after he died, I went to one of them *mediums* to try and get in contact with him.

Wishee (*interested*) And did you?

Twankey Of course I did. She went into one of her funny trances, and suddenly I heard his voice coming out of the darkness. "Titania," he said. "Oh, Cuthbert," I answered "Are you still in pain?" "No," he answered "I'm not in any pain." "Are you happy?" I asked him, and he said, "Yes ... I'm very happy." "Happier than you were when you were alive and with me?" I called back to him. "Oh, yes, Titania," he said. "Far, far happier." So I asked him what it was like up in Heaven. (*She pauses*) "Oh, I'm not in Heaven," he said.

Wishee Never mind, Mrs Twankey. It won't be long before you're married again. Here ... there's just one thing, though. I've never been married before and ... well ... I don't know how a husband behaves.

Twankey Oh, you don't have to let that worry you. There's nothing to it. Just watch the man in the house next door and do what he does. Every morning when he goes to work, he kisses his wife goodbye. Then he stands in the street and blows kisses to her for ten minutes and when he comes home at night, he kisses her "Hello". In fact . . . he kisses her every time he sees her. (*She smiles with pleasure at the thought of getting the same treatment*)

Wishee But I couldn't do that, Mrs Twankey. I don't even know the woman.

Song 14 (*Wishee and Twankey*)

At the end of the song they exit L

Aladdin and the Princess enter R

Aladdin Here we are, Princess. The gates of our new Palace.

Princess It's all happened so suddenly. Like some kind of dream. Even though we're married I can hardly believe it's true. Oh, Aladdin . . . how *did* you become so rich in such a short time? Did your uncle really take you to the place he mentioned?

Aladdin It's a long story, but I'll tell you all about it as soon as I return from the Market place. I want to give the poor people some money.

Princess (*smiling*) I'll await your return.

Aladdin turns to exit

Aladdin . . .

He turns to face her again

Why on earth are you carrying that dirty-looking old lamp with you?

Aladdin Oh . . . no particular reason. I'm just very fond of it, that's all.

Princess But it looks so silly fastened to the belt of your beautiful clothing. Please . . . leave it here at the Palace. I'll take care of it for you.

Aladdin (*hesitantly*) Well . . .

Princess Just to please me.

Aladdin Very well. (*He hands her the Lamp*) But take great care of it, I beg you.

Princess Don't worry. I will.

Aladdin gives her a cheery wave and exits

(*Calling*) Goodbye. (*She looks at the Lamp*) Now where can I put this for safety?

Abanazar (*off*) New lamps for old. New lamps for old.

So-Shy and the Handmaidens enter, giggling

Princess What is it? Why are you laughing?

So-Shy Listen, Your Highness.

Abanazar (*off*) New lamps for old. New lamps for old.

Princess (*amused*) New lamps for old? He must be mad.

Abanazar enters disguised as a lamp-seller. He carries a tall pole with crossbeams from which lamps are displayed

Abanazar New lamps for old . . .

Princess (*calling*) Excuse me. Just a moment. Did you *really* call out "New lamps for old", or am I dreaming?

Abanazar (*drawing close to her*) It is no dream, my dear. I am indeed offering a new lamp in exchange for an old one.

Princess (*bewildered*) Whatever for?

Abanazar The answer is simple, most beautiful lady. A lighted lamp is surely the most attractive object in any room. Think how the flickering flame reflects on the polished brass. How it sparkles and delights the eyes of true lovers . . .

Princess (*to the Handmaidens*) How very true.

Abanazar But when a lamp is old . . . and dirty . . . (*indicating her lamp*) . . . like *that* one . . . how can it reflect anything but a feeble glow? Why . . . it spoils the look of the whole room. Therefore . . . as a lover of beauty . . . I am offering a gleaming new lamp to anyone who thinks as I do.

Princess (*moved*) Oh, what a kind old gentleman you are.

Abanazar Would *you* care to inspect my lamps? (*He indicates his display*)

Princess (*uncertainly*) Well . . . I'm not sure. You see *this* lamp belongs to my husband and he's very fond of it. I'm not sure he'd want to part with it . . . even for one of *your* beautiful collection.

Abanazar Oh, I'm sure you're *wrong*, my dear. How can that dirty old thing compare with these delightful objects? Just *look* at them. (*He dangles the lamps invitingly*)

So-Shy (*drawing the Princess away*) Your Highness . . .

Princess (*protesting gently*) But they *are* beautiful, So-Shy. Oh, I'm sure Aladdin won't mind.

Abanazar (*closing in again*) Mind? He'll be delighted. You wait and see.

Princess (*suddenly*) Very well. Please change it for that one there. (*She indicates a lamp on the pole, and extends the magic one*)

Abanazar (*snatching the Lamp and tossing the lamp-rack aside*) At last. The Lamp is mine. (*He flings off his ragged cloak*) You gullible, gormless fool. (*He laughs harshly*)

The Princess and her Handmaidens react in dismay and bewilderment. Abanazar rubs the Lamp

> *There is a flash. The Genie appears*

Genie What is your wish, O master?

Princess (*distraught*) What have I done?

Abanazar (*to the Genie*) Transport this Palace and all it contains to far-off Egypt.

Genie It shall be done, O master.

Abanazar Come. (*He grabs hold of the Princess*) To the Land of the Sphinx. (*He begins to drag her off into the Palace*)

Princess (*struggling*) Aladdin. Aladdin. Help.

So-Shy flings herself at Abanazar who brushes her aside. She falls to the floor

> *Abanazar drags the Princess off*

The Handmaidens cluster around So-Shy with cries of concern. The Genie gives a sign. There is a Black-out and a crash of thunder

The Genie exits

All cry out in fear. The Lights come up again

There is a general entrance of Citizens, Courtiers, Slaves, the Emperor, the Vizier, Wishee, Twankey and Aladdin. The last three are all in rags again

Aladdin (*calling*) Princess. Princess. (*He looks down at his clothes*) My clothes . . . and the Palace . . . What's happened?
Emperor (*agitated*) Badroulbador. Badroulbador.
So-Shy (*raising herself*) Oh, Aladdin. Your Majesty. A horrible old magician came here disguised as a pedlar. He stole that dirty old lamp and kidnapped the Princess. Look . . . (*indicating upwards*) . . . your Palace is flying through the air on its way to Egypt.

All look up with groans of dismay and despair

Wishee Well . . . Egypt's not *too* bad. At least she won't be hungry.
Twankey Why not?
Wishee Because of all the sandwiches there.

Twankey hits him

Aladdin (*stricken*) It must have been Abanazar . . . and my Princess is in his evil hands. What can we do?
Emperor I'll tell you what you can do. You can get her back at once or I'll have your head chopped off.
Twankey Oh, blimey. He's back on his hobby-horse.
Aladdin Wait . . . there's just one chance. I still have the magic ring. (*He rubs it*)

There is a flash and the Slave of the Ring appears

O, Slave . . . dear Slave. Abanazar has stolen the Magic Lamp, my Princess, my Palace and all my possessions. Please help me get them back again.
Slave   I haven't the power to bring them back . . .
                   (*Smiling regretfully*)
                   But at least I can set you upon the right track.
                   After that, I'm afraid . . . well, it's up to you . . .
                   But I'm sure you'll succeed if your heart stays true.
Aladdin (*bravely*) Then point out the way to wherever they be.
Slave You ask . . . I obey. Please follow me.

All exit after the Slave with great excitement

The Lights fade rapidly for the end of the scene

SCENE 7

Egypt. Inside Aladdin's Palace

A great hall. Evening. Abanazar is sitting on an ornate throne dressed in rich clothing. He is being entertained by Dancing Girls in Egyptian-style clothing, and the Slaves in baggy silk trousers and stylized waistcoats are attending him. The Lamp is in his hands. When the dance ends, Abanazar rises

Abanazar Begone.

The Dancers exit quickly

Bring in the Princess Badroulbador.

Two Slaves quickly exit

(*Smirking*) How sweet the fruits of my triumph. Not only do I have the Magic Lamp, but the most beautiful creature on earth will soon be my bride. (*Leering*) I told you I'd win, didn't I?

The two Guards enter with the struggling Princess

Princess Let go of me. Let go. (*Calling*) Aladdin. Help.
Abanazar You'll have to shout louder than that, my sweet one. Aladdin is still in China.
Princess Don't speak to me, you repulsive brute.
Abanazar (*laughing*) Such language. Repulsive I may be ... but try to defy me and you'll soon learn your lesson. I can turn very ugly when I'm annoyed.
Princess Oh? And who's annoyed you tonight?
Abanazar (*sharply*) Have a care, pretty one. (*Relaxing*) At the moment I can understand you being a little upset ... but after we're *married*, I'm sure you'll see me in a new light.
Princess (*horrified*) Married? I'll *never* marry you.
Abanazar We shall see. You are my prisoner and cannot escape from here despite your puny efforts. I intend to marry you, come what may, so you'd better forget Aladdin and learn to love *me* instead.
Princess I'd rather die.
Abanazar (*smiling*) I'm sure you'll change your mind. (*To the Guards*) Take her away. A few moments alone with her thoughts, and I'm certain she'll reconsider.

The Guards drag the Princess away again

(*Moving down front*) How very strange. The Magic Lamp is mine and yet ... something tells me that all is not as it should be. Is it possible the boy Aladdin *could* find me and wrest it from my grasp? No, no. Imagination gets the better of me. (*He muses*) But even so ... A guardian I'll produce ... and whoever sets foot within these walls will feel the wrath of Abanazar. (*He raises his arms, mutters a few words and casts a spell*)

The Lights dim

Now let anyone try to steal my Lamp. (*To the Slaves*) Come.

Abanazar exits with his Slaves

As soon as he has gone, Wishee enters furtively

Wishee (*whispering*) Hiya kids. (*He glances round, then still looking off, backs* C, *in exaggerated fashion*)

The Emperor enters opposite, back to Wishee. He also moves C. *The two collide, react in terror, then turn and see each other*

(*Relieved*) Oh, Your Royal Magneticals. Thank goodness it's you.

Emperor (*nervously*) Oh, Wishee. What on earth's happened to this beautiful Palace? Back home in China it was splendid . . . but here in Egypt it all looks strange and frightening.

Wishee I know. I've got this funny feeling that hundreds of eyes are watching us.

Emperor That's the audience.

Wishee I wonder where Titania's got to?

Emperor And my Vizier.

Wishee (*pointing off*) Look. There she is. Swimming in the River Nile. (*Calling*) Titania. Come out of there at once.

Twankey (*off; faintly*) Whatever for? I'm enjoying myself.

Wishee (*calling*) That river's full of crocodiles.

Twankey enters

Twankey (*breathlessly*) Don't be silly. *I* never saw any crocodiles.

Wishee stares at the outrageous dress she is wearing

The Vizier enters opposite

Wishee Where on earth did you get *that* frock from?

Twankey Do you like it? I thought I'd better wear something special if I was visiting foreign countries.

Wishee It's a bit *tight*, isn't it?

Twankey Well . . . I wanted to wear something that would make *me* look slim . . . and *men* look round. (*She simpers*)

Vizier (*nervously to the Emperor*) Oh, I don't like it here, Your Majesty. I've a funny feeling the place is haunted.

Emperor (*sharply*) Don't be silly, Vizier. There's no such thing as a ghost.

Vizier With all due respect, sire . . . I beg to differ. I once stayed at a little country inn . . . and that was haunted by a terrible ghost. All night long it floated through the doors waking everyone up to ask for identification.

Wishee That wasn't a ghost. It was an Inn Spectre. (*He laughs*)

Twankey Well the Vizier's right. *I* don't like it here, either. There's something very strange about it.

Wishee Don't worry. If anything nasty creeps up on us, my pals out there in the audience will warn us . . . (*To the audience*) won't you?

Audience reaction

You see?

Twankey Well that's a relief, anyway. But what are we going to do while we're waiting for my Aladdin to find the Princess and get his Lamp back?

Emperor (*eagerly*) We could always have a little sing-song.

Vizier Oh, good idea. What shall we sing?

Twankey She was only a prizefighter's daughter ... but she certainly knew all the ropes.

Wishee Or, she was only a clergyman's daughter ... but she couldn't put anything pastor.

Emperor No, no, no. Let's sing "Nellie Dean". We *all* know *that*.

They begin to sing

As they do so, a Mummy lurches out of the shadows behind them

Wishee (*to the audience*) What's the matter?

Audience reaction

A *what*? (*To the others*) Somebody's mummy's behind us.

All laugh

Don't be silly, kids. All your mummies are sitting out there with you. They can't get up here. Honest.

Twankey (*amused*) Come on. Let's carry on singing.

They sing again. The Mummy comes closer. Audience reaction. They stop singing

Wishee (*calming the audience down*) All right. All right, then. We'll have a look and see if somebody's mummy *is* behind us.

They all march round. The Mummy tags on to the end of the line. Nothing sighted, the singers resume their line up and the Mummy stays behind them

Ah, you're pulling our legs. There's nobody there at all.

Audience reaction

Emperor (*crossly*) Now stop this nonsense at once. You're spoiling our song. Any more interruptions and I'll shorten the school holidays. (*To the others*) Come on, everyone. On with the singing.

They begin singing again. The Mummy clamps his hand on the Emperor's shoulder. The Emperor turns and sees it

The Emperor gives a loud shriek of fear and runs off

The Mummy moves back. Others stop singing

Twankey (*puzzled*) I never realized there was a top C in this song.

Wishee Here ... where's the Emperor gone?

All gaze about

Vizier (*calling nervously*) Your Majesty?

Twankey Oh, well. Never mind about him. There's still three of us. Let's go on with the song.

They sing. The Mummy clamps hold of the Vizier

The Vizier looks, screams and exits

The others stop singing

Wishee Here . . . he's gone now.
Twankey (*looking*) It's not time for the pubs to shut, is it? (*She brightens*)
Oh, well . . . we can sing just as nicely without them, can't we? They
weren't very good at harmonizing.
Wishee What's harmonizing?
Twankey The stuff you put on top of Christmas cakes. Sing.

They resume singing. The Mummy scares Wishee

Wishee screams and runs off

Twankey stops singing

(*Nervously*) Wishee? Wishee? Oh . . . I wishee'd come back. He's left me
all alone. On my own with nobody with me. I'd better keep singing and
stop myself from getting scared.

*She begins singing in a scared voice. The Mummy taps her on the shoulder. She
turns and sees it*

(*Puzzled*) I never noticed that mirror being there before.

*She peers closer, realizes, screams and dashes off madly, chased by the
Mummy*

As she exits, the Princess enters up R, *looking very dejected and tearful*

Princess Oh, Aladdin. Will I ever see you again. (*She sobs and moves* L)

Aladdin enters cautiously down R

Aladdin (*softly*) Princess.
Princess (*turning, startled*) Aladdin.

They hurry to each other

Oh, Aladdin. Thank goodness you're here. That awful old man is trying
to force me to marry him.
Aladdin (*warningly*) Shhh. He mustn't know I'm here. I've come to rescue
you, but first we have to get the Magic Lamp back and take away his
powers.
Princess But how?
Aladdin I have a plan. Call him into this room and make him think you've
changed your mind about marrying him. Then leave the rest to me.
(*Smiling*) Don't worry. Everything's going to be all right.

Aladdin exits

Princess (*calling temptingly*) Mr Abanazar.

Abanazar enters rapidly

Abanazar You called me, my little turtle dove?
Princess Why, yes. I've been thinking. If you *are* going to be Master of the
Universe, then I'd much rather be your Empress than stay just a Princess
of silly old China.

Abanazar (*delighted*) How very sensible of you, my dear. Come. Give me a tender squeeze. (*He reaches out for her*)

Aladdin springs out of hiding

Aladdin Abanazar ...

Abanazar spins round to face him with a snarl

Abracadabra, Abracadeez ... by the power of this ring I command you to freeze.

Abanazar freezes even as he is reaching for the Lamp

Princess (*amazed*) What's happened?

Aladdin (*laughing*) I've used one of the villain's own spells against him, that's all. What a good job he gave me his magic ring. (*He takes the Lamp from Abanazar*)

There is a general entrance of delighted people

And now to summon the Genie to take us all back home again. (*He rubs the Lamp*)

There is a flash and the Genie appears

Genie What is your wish, O master?

Aladdin Take this Palace and everyone in it, back to China.

Genie It shall be done, O master. (*He raises a hand*)

Twankey (*quickly*) Just a minute. Just a minute. What are we going to do about the Black Death, there? (*She indicates Abanazar*)

Emperor Oh, yes. We can't have him running around loose, can we?

Vizier Perhaps *I* could have him to practise on? I've invented a million new tortures I'd like to try out.

Wishee Here ... I've a good idea. Now that me and Titania are going to get married ... there's a certain laundry I know that'll be needing a new manager. How about making him start a new life with a clean sheet?

Aladdin (*delighted*) Good idea. I'll have the Genie arrange it as soon as we get back home. So everything's settled. Mr Genie ... to Peking as fast as you can.

Genie You order and I obey.

There is a loud cheer from all but Abanazar and an instant Black-out for the end of the scene

SCENE 8

Back in Peking. A lane scene

So-Shy enters carrying a card decorated with Chinese characters

So-Shy (*bowing politely*) Honourable guests. This humble handmaiden is pleased to draw your attention to this card. (*She displays it*)

Wishee enters

Wishee Hiya, kids. (*To So-Shy*) Hello, So-Shy. What are you doing?
So-Shy Hello, Wishee. Now is the moment that all have been waiting for?
  Honourable song-sheet. These are the words of our song, as written by
  the Emperor himself.
Wishee (*laughing*) Oh, it's no use you showing them *those* words. They
  don't understand them. The theatre's full of British people tonight. If
  we're going to have a song-sheet, we have to do it in *their* language.
  (*Thinking*) Now what songs do we know in English? I know . . .

*Wishee names the selected song and he and So-Shy conduct the song-sheet as
required*

Song 15

At the end of the song, Wishee and So-Shy exit at opposite sides

The Lights fade to Black-out as speedily as possible

SCENE 9

The Great Hall and Finale

As Scene 5. Full lighting

*A short dance is performed by Handmaidens who exit at once at the end of
the dance*

The walk-down begins as follows

Babes
Choristers
Slave of the Ring
Genie
So-Shy
Vizier
Emperor
Abanazar
Wishee
Twankey
Aladdin and Princess

Aladdin Our pantomime is over. Our story truly told.
Princess We hope you've all enjoyed *our* version of this legend old.
Wishee We've done our best to lift your hearts with dancing, song and
  laughter.
Twankey Good-night, God bless. And just like us . . . live happily ever after.

There is a reprise of any song in the show then——

the CURTAIN *falls*

FURNITURE AND PROPERTY LIST

ACT I

PROLOGUE

Personal: **Abanazar:** ring

On stage: Stalls *etc.*
Practical door to laundry

Off stage: Mop, wet sponge **(Girls)**
Notice **(Twankey)**
Scroll **(Vizier)**
Sedan chair **(Emperor** and **Slaves)**
Water wings, flippers, loofah **(Emperor)**
Sword **(Vizier)**

Personal: **Abanazar:** ring
Wishee: blindfold
Twankey: mirror in apron pocket
Emperor: fan
So-Shy: silk kerchief

SCENE 2

Off stage: Jug of water, funnel **(Twankey)**

Personal: **Abanazar:** ring
Vizier: 2 £1 notes, concealed hot-water bottle
Twankey: £1 note, 2p piece, concealed hot-water bottle
Wishee: 2 £1 notes, concealed hot-water bottle
Emperor: 2 £1 notes, concealed hot-water bottle

SCENE 3

On stage: Pavilion

Personal: **Abanazar:** ring

SCENE 4

No props required

SCENE 5

On stage: Washing machine (*see Production Note on page v*)
Large box washing powder

Blackboard, easel, chalk, duster
2 baskets of dirty washing including bloomers with padlock and chain,
  bloomers made from flag, stockings with no feet, long johns
Other laundry items (for **Dancers**)

Off stage: Darning box with needle and thread, scissors, stool **(Twankey)**
Box washing powder **(Babe)**

Personal: **Wishee:** L plate

SCENE 6

On stage: Large boulder

Personal: **Abanazar:** ring

SCENE 7

On stage: Rocks
Lamp on small rock

Personal: **Aladdin:** ring

ACT II

SCENE 1

On stage: Streamers, lanterns (for **Dancers**)

Off stage: Bunch of flowers, shopping bag **(Wishee)**
Lamp **(Aladdin)**

Personal: **Emperor:** fan
Aladdin: ring

SCENE 2

No props required

SCENE 3

On stage: As Act I, Scene 5

Personal: **Aladdin:** sack of jewels, ring, lamp on belt

SCENE 4

On stage: Dressing as required

Personal: **Princess:** handkerchief

SCENE 5

On stage: Throne
Cushion

Off stage: Gold, silver dishes with jewels *etc.* **(Babes, Slaves)**

Personal: **Aladdin:** ring, lamp on belt

SCENE 6

Off stage: Tall pole with lamps **(Abanazar)**

Personal: **Aladdin:** ring, lamp on belt

SCENE 7

On stage: Throne
Lamp (for **Abanazar**)

Off stage: Lamp **(Abanazar)**

Personal: **Aladdin:** ring

SCENE 8

Off stage: Song-sheet **(So-Shy)**

SCENE 9

On stage: As Act II, Scene 5

Personal: **Aladdin:** ring, lamp on belt

LIGHTING PLOT

Property fittings required: *nil*

Various interior and exterior settings

ACT I, Prologue

To open: Dim blue and green lighting; green spot on **Abanazar**

Cue 1   **Slave:** "... of Old Peking."   (Page 2)
        Black-out

ACT I, Scene 1

To open: Bright, general lighting

Cue 2   **Aladdin** and **Twankey** exit into laundry   (Page 5)
        Dim lights; bring up green spot on **Abanazar**

Cue 3   **Abanazar** exits   (Page 5)
        Cut green spot; return lights to previous level

Cue 4   **Police** and **Guards** rush after **Aladdin**   (Page 14)
        Black-out

ACT I, Scene 2

To open: General lighting

Cue 5   **Emperor** chases **Twankey** off in a temper   (Page 18)
        Black-out

ACT I, Scene 3

To open: Bright, general lighting

Cue 6   **Abanazar** gives harsh laugh and exits   (Page 20)
        Quick fade to Black-out

ACT I, Scene 4

To open: General lighting

Cue 7   **Wishee** and **Babes** march off cheerfully   (Page 21)
        Fade to Black-out

ACT I, Scene 5

To open: Bright, general lighting

Cue 8   **Twankey** faints into **Aladdin**'s arms   (Page 25)
           Black-out

ACT I, SCENE 6

To open: Subdued lighting

Cue 9   **Wishee** enters   (Page 25)
           Spot on him

Cue 10   **Wishee** exits and **Abanazar** enters   (Page 26)
           Cut spot on **Wishee**; *green spot on* **Abanazar**

Cue 11   **Abanazar** moves c   (Page 27)
           Fade lights down to spot on **Abanazar**'s *face and shoulders*

Cue 12   **Abanazar:** "Abanazar ..." (*1st time*)   (Page 27)
           Fade spot to Black-out

ACT I, SCENE 7

To open: Blue, green, red lighting; light shining down through entrance

Cue 13   **Abanazar:** "... hold him fast for evermore."   (Page 28)
           Cut light shining through entrance

Cue 14   **Genie** makes sign   (Page 30)
           Sunlight streams in through cave entrance

ACT II, SCENE 1

To open: Bright general lighting

Cue 15   **Genie** makes a signal   (Page 36)
           Black-out

Cue 16   When ready   (Page 36)
           Return to previous lighting

Cue 17   As **Aladdin** sings Song 10   (Page 36)
           Gradually fade to spot on **Aladdin**'s *head and shoulders*

Cue 18   At end of Song 10   (Page 36)
           Black-out

ACT II, SCENE 2

To open: Bright general lighting

Cue 19   **All** exit   (Page 37)
           Quick fade to Black-out

ACT II, SCENE 3

To open: Bright general lighting

Cue 20   **Twankey** finishes comic strip-tease   (Page 40)
           Black-out

ACT II, SCENE 4

To open: Soft interior lighting

Cue 21   **Princess** exits slowly and sadly   (Page 40)
                Fade to Black-out

ACT II, SCENE 5

To open: Bright general lighting

Cue 22   **Aladdin** and the **Princess** step forward   (Page 42)
                Begin to fade lighting; bring up spots on **Aladdin** *and* **Princess** *as
                they separate; fade other lighting*

Cue 23   At end of Song 13   (Page 42)
                Fade spots to Black-out

ACT II, SCENE 6

To open: General lighting

Cue 24   **Abanazar** enters   (Page 42)
                Dim lighting

Cue 25   **Twankey** and **Wishee** enter   (Page 43)
                Return to previous level

Cue 26   **Genie** gives sign   (Page 45)
                Black-out

Cue 27   When ready   (Page 46)
                Bring up general lighting

Cue 28   **All** exit after the **Slave**   (Page 46)
                Fade to Black-out

ACT II, SCENE 7

To open: Dim interior lighting

Cue 29   **Abanazar** casts spell   (Page 47)
                Dim lighting further

Cue 30   **All** cheer   (Page 5)
                Black-out

ACT II, SCENE 8

To open: Full general lighting

Cue 31   **Wishee** and **So-Shy** exit   (Page 52)
                Quick fade to Black-out

ACT II, SCENE 9
To open: Full general lighting
No cues

EFFECTS PLOT

ACT I

Cue 1	**Abanazar** rubs ring *Flash as* **Slave** *appears*	(Page 1)
Cue 2	**Vizier:** ". . . Emperor of China." *Loud discordant fanfare*	(Page 10)
Cue 3	**Abanazar** rubs ring *Flash as* **Slave** *appears*	(Page 15)
Cue 4	**Abanazar** casts spell over boulder *Rumble as boulder rolls to one side*	(Page 26)
Cue 5	**Abanazar:** ". . . hold him fast for evermore." *Flash and loud rumble as entrance is sealed*	(Page 28)
Cue 6	**Aladdin** rubs ring *Flash as* **Slave** *appears*	(Page 28)
Cue 7	**Aladdin** rubs lamp *Flash and crack of thunder as* **Genie** *appears*	(Page 29)

ACT II

Cue 8	**Aladdin** rubs lamp *Flash as* **Genie** *appears*	(Page 35)
Cue 9	**Twankey** rubs lamp *Flash as* **Genie** *appears*	(Page 38)
Cue 10	**Abanazar** rubs lamp *Flash as* **Genie** *appears*	(Page 45)
Cue 11	**Genie** gives sign *Crash of thunder*	(Page 45)
Cue 12	**Aladdin** rubs ring *Flash as* **Slave** *appears*	(Page 46)
Cue 13	**Aladdin** rubs lamp *Flash as* **Genie** *appears*	(Page 51)

MADE AND PRINTED IN GREAT BRITAIN BY
LATIMER TREND & COMPANY LTD PLYMOUTH
MADE IN ENGLAND

Milton Keynes UK
Ingram Content Group UK Ltd.
UKHW022024270224
438573UK00019B/344